DISMISSED

D1714632

DISMISSED

HOW MEDIA AGENDAS AND JUDICIAL BIAS CONSPIRE TO UNDERMINE JUSTICE

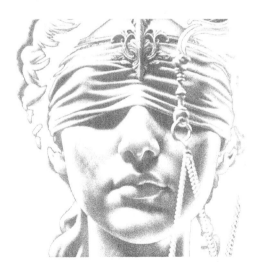

TODD MCMURTRY
WITH JD STEVENSON

GHIKA BOOKS

First Edition Paperback, 2024

This book contains information regarding legal topics and legal proceedings. The information is not advice and should not be treated as such. While the author and publisher have made every effort to ensure that the information in this book was correct at press time, the author and publisher do not assume and hereby disclaim any liability to any party for any loss, damage, or disruption caused by errors or omissions, whether such errors or omissions result from negligence, accident, or any other cause.

This book is intended as a general guide only and should not be relied upon as legal advice. Readers should consult with a qualified attorney for advice on specific legal issues related to their situation. The cases and circumstances discussed in this book are intended as illustrative examples only and should not be considered a prediction of future events or outcomes.

The views expressed in this book are those of the author alone and should not be attributed to any court or legal body with which the author may be affiliated.

Unless otherwise indicated, all Scripture quotations are from The ESV® Bible (The Holy Bible, English Standard Version®), © 2001 by Crossway, a publishing ministry of Good News Publishers. Used by permission. All rights reserved.

Book & Cover Design by Ghika Books

ISBN 979-8-32-725235-6 (amzn pbk.)

I dedicate this book first and foremost to my wife, Maria C. "Cari" Garriga. We have been married for over 35 years. She has stood by me through good times and bad. I would not have made it without her.

I also want to thank the hundreds of people I have represented over the years. By helping good people through tough times, I have learned so much about the human character. Good people always survive the most severe traumas. Their faith in God and their families support them as they go through tough times. They have taught me how to listen, how to empathize, and how to help move people from a place of vulnerability to reconciliation. My sacrifices for them, and theirs for me, have made me a better person who hopes he has just a bit of wisdom to share with the world.

Contents

1. Answering the Call 1
Why I Started Fighting an Impossible Foe

2. Meet Defamation 17
America's Hidden Plague

3. Nobody is Safe 41
Defamation's Impact on the Citizen

4. Fact and Opinion 65
The Truth Will Set You Free? Don't Be So Naive

5. Your Silence is Their Goal 85
The Anatomy of a Media Hit Job

6. Burning Down the Platform 113
How Media and Big Tech Silence Opposition

7. Law is a Battlefield 137
The Weaponization of "Justice"

8. Removing the Blindfold of Justice 155
When Judges Get Political

9. A House Built on Sand 179
The Basis of Modern Defamation Law

10. Asleep at the Wheel   **193**
   Old Laws and Mob Rule

11. Unsettled Issues   **217**
   Wandering the Wasteland Without Landmarks

12. We Must Win   **245**
   Standing Strong for Our Future

Don't Be Dismissed   **255**
   What to Do When You Are in the Crosshairs

Glossary of Important Terms   **265**

Bibliography   **269**

ANSWERING THE CALL

WHY I STARTED FIGHTING
AN IMPOSSIBLE FOE

"The good lawyer is not the man who has an eye to every side and angle
of contingency, and qualifies all his qualifications, but who throws
himself on your part so heartily, that he can get you out of a scrape."
- Ralph Waldo Emerson

Excellence, in the McMurtry house, was a way of life. My mother, Jeannine VanDerVeer, was a force of nature. Descended from General Ferdinand VanDerVeer of the Union Army, she was always on the move—be it restoring historic homes in Covington, Kentucky, serving as a trauma nurse, or founding a tobacco company. She ensured my brother and I stayed out of trouble as she relentlessly stood by my father's side, who called her his "Shield Maiden." Then there was my father, Stephen McMurtry. Famously, he had very few hobbies. Law, home restorations, and presiding over his family were his passions.

In law, he served for over thirty years as the lawyer for the city of Covington, much of that during a time when the city had no insurance. He's been credited with virtually single-handedly keeping Covington out of bankruptcy. During the 1980s and 1990s, he won twenty straight jury verdicts for the city. Even though he worked primarily for the city (and the Housing Authority of Covington), he was known throughout the community as a friend to all. An early memory of mine is overhearing two people at the public library, both appearing to be homeless, discussing some troubles one of them was having. After listening to his friend, the other said, "You should really go see Stephen McMurtry. He will help you."

The ethics of my family were straightforward and undeniable. Be truthful, stand up for your fellow man, be equal parts tough and distinguished—and, in order to uphold these values, go against the grain as often as necessary. Given how my parents lived, it would have been impossible for me not to etch these principles into my core. While I was the child of a lawyer, my upbringing in Covington was alongside an incredibly diverse group of people. Much of that was because my parents were so involved in helping restore areas wracked with poverty and hardship.

Law, it seemed, was a constant presence in my house. My father's office was nearby, and I remember a steady stream of lawyers being frequent guests while my parents played gracious hosts. Inevitably, case law, courtroom strategy, dealings with opposing counsel, and the behavior of certain judges would lead to long debates into the night. My father often served as the final word—his knowledge and confident demeanor proved too much for most guests.

When I graduated from high school at sixteen, I didn't feel an urge to go straight to college. I didn't want to shove my face in a book; I wanted to experience life. So, I enrolled in a couple of part-time classes at Northern Kentucky University and began working at Bonanza Steakhouse—a well-known, family-oriented series of restaurants situated in both Ohio and Kentucky. I started as a dishwasher, but within less than a year, I became the "Head Grill Man"—a position that allowed me to visit multiple Bonanza restaurants in the area where I was the Chief Instructor on grilling steaks.

Looking back, I don't think my amazing cooking skills landed me that job. What enabled me to succeed was my ability to carry myself with authority, clearly communicate ideas, and understand the needs of people. When the time came for me to officially leave for college, I was offered a more prominent role with the restaurant—a tempting offer that I often reflect on to this day. Just one small decision change and I may be the proud owner of a series of Chipotle or Chick-fil-A establishments. But that's another story for another time.

Instead, I headed off to Centre College in Danville, Kentucky. I was the third generation of my family to attend Centre College. My time as an undergraduate was both fun and informative. Leaning on my desire not only to gain knowledge but experience as well, I joined a fraternity, was an active member of the swim team, studied when necessary (but didn't allow myself to stress over maintaining a perfect GPA), worked two jobs in the summer, and tried to soak up the college experience as much as possible. As graduation approached, I decided to go straight into law school. For me, it was a natural next step; having grown up around my father's practice, I got to see firsthand how much he was able to help people and how respected he was due to his position. And, having known so many other lawyers, it was clear that most were genuine, hard-working, and ethical people.

Law school at the Salmon P. Chase College of Law was a very different experience than when I obtained my undergraduate degree. There was a much more competitive dynamic at play among my classmates—it was clear that many of my contemporaries were looking to land a job with some gigantic firm or had watched Paul Newman in *The Verdict* one too many times. I never felt at home in that program, which likely caused me to not engage in the experience the same way I had while an undergraduate. Don't get me wrong, I didn't flunk out—in fact, I did just fine academically, even passing the Bar Exam on my first try—but I also wasn't "all in."

My father, being of the old-school mindset that a young man needs to support himself, decided to stop assisting me financially after I acquired my undergraduate degree (I respect him for making that decision). I again found myself balancing academics and working, this time for my father or other lawyers I knew, doing research, clerking, or any other jobs that needed to be done. Not only did that support me through law school, but it was an invaluable deeper look into the workings of law firms—something I value to this day. I also made some good friends and learned from various small-firm and solo-practice lawyers. These are lawyers closest to the people who best understand justice.

Toward the end of my tenure in law school, I was set up on a blind date. Tending to hold these things with a pretty open hand, I went into the interaction, hoping, at minimum, to have an enjoyable evening with a new person. Fate had other plans. I found myself sitting across the table from the most beautiful, intelligent, witty, and gracious young lady I could have imagined. She was from Puerto Rico and was in the U.S. to attend graduate school at the University of Cincinnati. I couldn't take my eyes off her. Lucky for me, the feeling was mutual. Just a few months later, Cari and I were engaged. About 18 months later, we were married, and law school was in my rearview mirror. Life was rushing into the future, and I was holding on for dear life.

There aren't many instances I recall where my father sat me down to offer drawn-out speeches about self-improvement or advice about the path my life should take. He wasn't that type of mentor—his mentorship came through how he lived his life, not the speeches he made about how to live life. But I remember one very specific bit of advice he gave me as my time in law school was coming to an end: "Don't go straight into law."

That guidance struck a chord with me, so Cari and I packed up and moved to Washington, D.C. Politics fascinated me as far back as high school when I won awards in speech and debate competitions under the tutelage of Father Paul Arbogast. I loved the power of a persuasive speech as much as the rush I felt on stage delivering it. Politics, or a career adjacent to the political arena, felt like the right move if I wasn't going to practice law.

Once in D.C., I landed a job with the Republican National Committee, working for the Finance Committee, fundraising, and helping to build a stronger Republican foundation in the 1980s. Working there was pure adrenaline. The stakes were high; my colleagues were the best at their jobs, and I was rolling right along with them. However, it didn't take me long to understand politics is itinerant in nature. When one party is in power, the folks aligned with that party are flush with work. But when the tides turn, those same folks are out, and there's a new crop on the other side to take their place. I also began to understand that to have power, you need to either be rich or get elected—but all too often, once you're elected, you're controlled by the rich folks. This dynamic seems more true than ever in today's America. Sadly, this is one of the reasons I'm writing this book.

Ultimately, Cari and I decided to head back to Covington. We were new parents, and I felt the draw not only back to my hometown but back to law. The first few years back, I worked in my father's firm. My dad's character remained true to form—he gave me no handouts, and any advice was rare. But I watched him. And I watched other lawyers. I took note when a judge commented on how immaculate another lawyer's brief was or how my father carried himself while litigating. We worked together on a few cases where I saw firsthand how strategic and thoughtful he was for his clients.

That same ethic of excellence ingrained in me throughout my entire life took more profound root as I built my own practice. I've been fortunate to be named a Super Lawyer in both Ohio and Kentucky for many years. In 2019, I was rated one of the top 50 lawyers in Kentucky—this is out of 20,000 licensed attorneys. My children have grown into fabulous adults and parents. I've currently been married to my lovely wife for over 37 years.

Like my father before me, life as a lawyer in Covington, Kentucky, has been a fantastic journey. And yet, a shadow has begun to creep alongside me in recent years. While the law of the United States has been my companion as far back as I can remember, how the law is being adjudicated feels less familiar to me. This has brought me to a crossroads recently. My first defamation case became a national sensation almost overnight—I found myself in a true baptism by fire. What stood out the most was how unjust the whole situation was. There were times of overwhelming stress and uncertainty. But in those moments, I was brought back to the ethics of my parents.

Be truthful, stand up for your fellow man, be equal parts tough and distinguished—and, in order to uphold these values, go against the grain as often as necessary.

We need to go against the grain now more than ever.

Visit virtually any civics class across our country (if it hasn't been taken over by some outlandish new teaching theory or activist teacher), and you are likely to hear terms like "Three Branches of Government" and "A System of Checks and Balances" when discussing the Constitution of the United States of America. You will hear teachers lauding that our three branches of government were set up to ensure no single person or group of people could become too powerful. If the instructor feels especially inspired, the lesson will undoubtedly be paired with a reminder that our Founding Fathers set this system in place because they never wanted these United States to fall into the same corrupt despotism and aristocratic rule from which they had just won their freedom.

A branch to make laws (Legislative), a branch to enforce laws (Executive), and a branch to ensure the laws are constitutional (Judicial). Powerful enough to enable the creation and growth of the greatest nation on earth. Simple enough that a middle school student can understand it. Precise and effective. One may go so far as to say elegant—constitutional engineering at its finest.

It's easy to understand why our government's legislative and executive branches receive the most news coverage. Emotionally charged political campaigns, outspoken candidates that promise a better life if they win, and round-the-clock monitoring of polling stations at election time—it has become the stuff of reality television and makes for great debate on a Saturday morning at local breakfast spots in the smallest towns or the biggest cities. There's an ebb and flow to the process, and there's always a side against which to root. Don't get me wrong; these two branches' work is essential. However, depending on the political winds of the time, some of these representatives can be given to such passion that they begin to bump against the Constitution and how it applies to our world in the early 21st Century. It is in these moments that the judicial branch proves its worth.

All biases aside, given my chosen profession, I consider the judicial branch of our government to play the most crucial role in keeping the United States aligned with the principles outlined in our Constitution. As I write this, it seems we are in one of the most turbulent political seasons in our nation's history. The divide between party lines (and even within parties) appears to widen on a daily basis. Emotions are at an all-time high in the halls of Congress and across the way at 1600 Pennsylvania Avenue. With high emotion comes inflated rhetoric and the desire to win a political battle at all costs. These are the times in which the judicial branch must stand firm. It must stand, in as many ways as possible, separated from the politics of the other two branches. The judicial branch and the justices who fill it must be the cliffs against which the political tide crashes—always standing strong to ensure the Constitution remains the final say in how our country is governed.

Revisiting the Story of Tom Sawyer

I recently re-read Mark Twain's classic, *Tom Sawyer*. Putting any controversy aside regarding character names or phonetic dialog, I was struck in a new way by one of the book's most well-known and often-referenced scenes. In the second chapter, while we're getting to know Tom, we watch him internally lament the task he's been given to paint his aunt's fence. While he struggles to muster the will to paint the fence, he prepares himself for the inevitable mockery he will receive from his peers as they pass by—they are enjoying a luxurious day free from responsibility, yet he is shackled with the consequences of previous poor decisions. We know too well what happens next. Tom hatches a plan to make himself the envy of his friends by showing the joy of fence painting. Before long, we see Tom sitting comfortably in the shade as friend after friend not only performs labor on his behalf but bribes him with trinkets and goodies for the honor. Oh, what a clever young lad, this Tom Sawyer.

But what of his "friends"? One by one, they inherit the task of fence painting only to work themselves to exhaustion. Ultimately, they are left lighter in their pocket, calorie deficient, and realizing they have wasted a day full of such possibilities. I imagine them waking the next day with sunburnt necks, sore arms, and paint-stained clothing, wondering what terrible spell had been cast to cause them to act so foolishly. They fell prey to a sort of hallucination that had them all agreeing that up was suddenly down and left was somehow right. The only beneficiary was a cavalier young Mr. Sawyer, who decided to turn reality on its head for the sake of a relaxing afternoon and a few useless objects.

Oh, come now, one may say, *who are we to say different? After all, Tom didn't hold a gun to their heads—nobody had to paint that silly fence.* Fair enough. But let's say those same kids didn't wake up the next morning having shaken Tom's manipulation from their heads. Let's imagine instead that they woke up, stretched their arms, found new clothes, gathered another marble, and marched over to Tom's house, offering their bribe, and asking which fence they should paint today. And imagine they did this day after day, week after week, and so on until they knew nothing more than fence painting and trinket offering. Imagine if the lie became so entrenched that the truth was no longer considered a possibility. *The Adventures of Tom Sawyer* would be a much darker and depressing story.

Sadly, in today's United States, I fear we may be waking up in a reality where we have been fed a lie that has so permeated our understanding of truth that we are on the brink of not being able to understand the world our Forefathers sought to build when crafting our judicial system and its role as gatekeeper for the American citizen. Year after year, we find ourselves standing by as our three branches of government are being blurred together into one—and we're being left on the sidelines to fend for ourselves as the two main political parties vie for their agendas to take over the judicial branch.

It has become an all too familiar refrain over the last few presidential elections: "The next sitting president will have the opportunity to appoint Supreme Court Justices who may change the landscape of the United States for decades to come." This power is not limited to appointing members of the Supreme Court. In fact, an average of one hundred sixty federal justices are appointed over the course of every four-year term. And with each appointment comes the inevitable discussion regarding the presumptive judge's political leaning. It's as if we have thrown our hands in the air and accepted that if a Republican appoints a justice, said justice will lean conservative with each ruling, either due to an implied loyalty or strongly held bias. Or if appointed by a Democrat, the justice will carte blanche impose a liberal agenda while wielding the gavel. And, on the off chance a justice decides to "cross party lines" with a ruling, there's an almost audible gasp across the arena of political pundits. What should be commonplace is treated as an astonishing break in form.

So, the question becomes, what do we do? How do we put down the proverbial brushes and tell Mr. Sawyer that he can paint his own fence, thank you very much—we've got a swimming hole to visit! From a macro point of view, this issue may seem just too daunting. I began asking this question in earnest a few years back when I started representing a high school student from my hometown of Covington, Kentucky, as he was thrown into the national spotlight over a viral video of him and his classmates while they were on a trip to Washington, D.C. This young man's name is Nick Sandmann, and his case caught the attention of celebrities, pundits, average citizens, and politicians alike. Overnight, this young man became the topic for shows on virtually every major news network as talking heads weighed in about the situation in which Nick found himself on that fateful Friday afternoon on the steps of the Lincoln Memorial. And as different points of view began to form, the attacks on Nick's character began.

Narratives were crafted, and defamatory claims about Nick's behavior, intentions, and perspectives were presented as fact. Colleges said Nick and his fellow Covington Catholic students should be denied college admissions. Alumni reported to me that they removed the school from their resumes. Nick Sandmann was becoming a household name for all the wrong reasons. The political punditry was in full swing, and this young man had unwillingly become the figure around whom both sides were forming their arguments. And it was destroying his life.

The ensuing legal battle I fought on behalf of Mr. Sandmann proved both daunting and educational. It was a battle fought on multiple fronts, against multiple interests. The media conglomerates had armies of highly paid and deeply connected lawyers. Public opinion continued to be fueled by celebrity hot takes. Some pundits were more than happy to use my client's situation as a springboard for more views and higher dollars. Those were difficult enough foes.

However, as the case progressed, it became apparent that current defamation laws were so dated and deformed that they could not rightly adjudicate the 21st century's technological, social, and political dynamics. In short, for Mr. Sandmann (and many of my other clients suffering from life-altering defamation wrongs), it would take a careful and measured approach to how constitutional principles such as freedom of speech and a person's right to a good reputation are impacted by things like social media and TV personalities who operate closer to the realm of opinion than fact. Add to this a corporate media establishment that has hoodwinked legislatures across the county to pass laws providing outrageous protections to multibillion-dollar companies, and we now confront an environment so hostile to the common person that it seems hopeless.

My intent for the ensuing chapters of this book is to take an unblinking look at the legal and judicial landscape through

the lens of defamation law. The topic is not a simple one—
there are complexities in defamation cases that shine a
spotlight on the need for a clear and unbiased justice system.
It is my hope that as we work our way through what
defamation is, how it impacts the lives of those against which
it is used, and the inadequacies we see in current laws that are
being applied, we will come to understand how vital it is for
our justice system to recast and reimagine the law in a
manner that protects you, me, friends, and relatives from this
unjust legal regime.

MEET DEFAMATION

AMERICA'S HIDDEN PLAGUE

"Like a madman who throws firebrands, arrows, and death is the man who deceives his neighbor and says, 'I am only joking!'"
- Proverbs 26:18-19

Downtown Covington, situated just across the Ohio River from Cincinnati, is a perfect mixture of urban night scene and slightly gentrified elegance. Whether you're looking for an intimate celebration dinner for two or a live music party with friends, you can find exactly what you want. Being a popular starting point for what the Kentucky Distillers Association calls The Bourbon Trail[1] (a catchy and tourist-friendly moniker for the dense collection of whiskey distilleries in Central Kentucky), the selection of unique and rare whiskey is abundant.

Walking down Covington's main street, Madison Avenue, one can't help but be reminded that this place is rich in history. Most of the buildings proudly display the pre-Civil

War date of their completion etched in fine brickwork over doorways or on commemoration plaques. This old-meets-new ambiance drew my wife and me for a date on a January evening in 2019.

Once seated, drinks on the way, and having given our appetizer selection, I excused myself to use the restroom. Upon returning, my wife was scrolling on her phone—something, it seemed, had caught her eye. We're not one of those couples who go out to dinner and spend the whole meal with our noses buried in our phones, which made the intensity of her focus even more intriguing. Over the next few minutes, she briefly described an altercation that had taken place in Washington, D.C., between a group of high school students and some protestors earlier in the day. I followed her lead, opened X (back then, it was still Twitter), and took my first step into the proverbial rabbit hole that changed the course of my life from that moment on.

Most know what happened while a group of high school students waited for a bus as the Indigenous People's March was ending near the Lincoln Memorial. Two individuals, one high school student (Nick Sandmann) and one member of the Omaha Tribe (Nathan Phillips), came face-to-face while a small group from a third party shouted insults at passers-by. It was an emotionally charged scene. While Mr. Sandmann and Mr. Phillips stood face-to-face, Phillips beating his drum inches from Sandmann's face and even touching his collar, a crowd gathered, each side shouting, singing, and dancing. In the midst of it all, phone cameras jostled to capture the moment.

Not long after, a one-minute-long clip from one of those phone recordings was uploaded to Twitter, accusing Mr. Sandmann of blocking the march in which Mr. Phillips was participating, acting disrespectfully, and taunting the members of the march. Shortly after, this video was re-posted to Twitter, quickly gaining millions of views. More clips were posted, showing various angles of the altercation, each with its own contextualization.

Most of the framing of Mr. Sandmann and his schoolmates in a negative light is due, in part, to the Make America Great Again hat he wore and the way he was smiling while face-to-face with Mr. Phillips. In what seemed like a matter of minutes, these videos were being re-posted to every conceivable social channel. News outlets took notice. Celebrities began weighing in. As heightened as the emotions were at the Lincoln Memorial, the response across the nation skyrocketed.

There I sat in the middle of dinner, my food barely eaten, as I watched the conversation unfold on my phone. I could barely keep up with the flood of posts—each time I refreshed the screen; it seemed more people were jumping into the conversation, an overwhelming majority of which were decrying their perception of Mr. Sandmann's behavior. Dinner ended, and we returned home, where I continued to watch the nation align around the initial narrative. I could not believe my eyes. It was as if I was sitting in the same movie theater, watching a different movie than everyone else.

As I dug deeper into newer posts with alternate video clips, I began to see a very different scene than what almost everyone else saw. I wasn't in the habit of posting to social media very much, but at some point in the evening, I felt the need to engage.

It could be a simple case of me seeing a vastly different scene than others. That was undoubtedly part of it. But I was also overcome by how close to home it was hitting for me. Mr. Sandmann, as it turned out, wasn't just a random high school student. He attended Covington Catholic High School—a school in my hometown. My youngest son went there. To me, he was just a kid who found himself in a bizarre situation and was being thrown into the national spotlight. If this had happened decades earlier, this could have been me. If just a few years earlier, it could have been one of my own children. *How*, I asked myself, *could this spin out of control so quickly?*

Moderation had been lost. Barely twelve hours after the confrontation, the students of Covington Catholic High School were being decried as insensitive, threatening, racist—

the list went on and on. Some called for them to be re-educated to be more sensitive. Even the mayor of Covington condemned the encounter. And Nick Sandmann's face was plastered alongside each accusation.

The speed at which the story took off made it evident to me that this went far beyond a general reaction to a minor confrontation in Washington, D.C. Given the political rhetoric at play across our nation, this seemed like a rallying cry behind which certain political groups could gather. Nick Sandmann quickly lost his humanity in the conversation. Instead, it appeared that the more he could be made into a monster, the further certain viewpoints could be broadcast. It felt wrong. And no matter how much I watched or the few times I engaged to offer my perspective, I began to realize how outmatched Nick was. This shouldn't be allowed. The claims being made, the quick reactions and fervent admonitions against Nick certainly couldn't be allowed to stand. The strong sense of justice under which I was raised, as well as my standing as a lawyer, had awakened in me a desire to step from behind the keyboard and into the fight.

While getting ready for bed that night, I was overwhelmed with the sense that I would be part of helping Nick through this. The feeling was so strong that I shared it with my wife. The feeling came true the next day when Nick's family contacted me, and I became his legal counsel.

This was the genesis of my journey into defamation law. A journey that has allowed me to represent national figures and everyday citizens alike. Each new case reminds me of how important it is to keep fighting for those who have faced the loss of jobs, death threats, financial ruin, doxing, and so much more due to having their reputation maligned.

What is Defamation Anyway?

I want to use this chapter to lay the groundwork for a shared vernacular as we progress through our examination of both the current state of defamation law, and the ways our justice system is being hijacked by political bias—often at the hands of large corporations, high-powered celebrities, and media conglomerates. As we progress, I want us to understand that, as much as we'd like to believe there are clear-cut legal definitions and categories for most situations, the truth is quite different. Most times, there are gray areas in the law. When it comes to defamation, the gray areas are vast, which is why it is so easy for bad actors to hide behind outdated laws, slippery slope arguments, misapplied precedents, or politically motivated justices. To fully unpack these ideas, let's start at the beginning—I've been told that's a very good place to start.

The simplest definition of defamation from Merriam-Webster's dictionary could not be more straightforward:

The act of communicating false statements about a person that injure the reputation of that person[2]

The concept is ancient, and in many world religions, the gods and central spiritual figures must often endure false statements made about them that impugn their character and intentions. In fact, by the third Chapter of Genesis, the opening book of the Jewish and Christian Bible, we see God enduring defamation shortly after we are told the story of creation. Many pantheistic religions, including Hinduism, Greek, Roman, and Norse mythologies, regularly depict the gods defaming one another to their fellow deities and humanity. Claiming falsehoods about someone, to the harm of their reputation, is an ancient game, to say the least.

Historically, there have been two methods of defaming someone: either through speech (slander) or through a physical act like writing, drawing, statues, etc. (libel). As technology creates more and more mediums for communication, this definition can blur; indeed, it has sometimes been noted to devolve into almost arbitrary categories.[3] How should the law treat a written Facebook post with a libelous title and a slanderous video? At the core, we have our words and deeds in this life, and if either of those falsely represents the people around us to their reputational harm, then we have engaged in "defamation."

As simple as defamation law might be to define conceptually, its practical application has become exceptionally complex. Thousands of previous common law rulings, combined with the rules of each jurisdiction and the balance of free speech guaranteed by the First Amendment, all work together to create a vast, complicated ocean of details, caveats, and definitions. But the goal of what it seeks to protect is fundamental.

Defamation law, despite its intricate doctrines, is fundamentally about balancing elemental values. It recognizes the importance of free information flow in a vibrant society, but insists on remedies for harmful lies. It stands at the crossroads of protecting reputation against baseless slander and upholding free speech and lively debate, which are essential to democracy.[4]

As with any topic rooted in our Bill of Rights, it is hotly debated by proponents with strongly differing views. It runs the risk of being corrupted by special interests, abused by large corporate interests, and co-opted by activism so that it can be aimed at the very people it was meant to protect. Sadly, to some degree, we have seen all of this occur in today's society. In the coming years, how we treat laws around defamation will not only inform future legal decisions, but also have the potential to impact just what it means to be an "American" who can engage in free speech while at the same time protecting our right to a good reputation.

The Legal Complexities of Defamation

The average person may find their head spinning as they try to understand what "defamation" really means legally. If you find yourself in this place, take heart, as even the most seasoned experts can find it confusing. Rodney A. Smolla, the author of one of the seminal works on defamation law (who has served as counsel for several notable cases), openly states, "There is no way succinctly to state the elements of a modern cause of action for defamation..."[5] There are too many factors when considering the people involved, the nature and medium of communication, jurisdictions, circumstances, and the ever-growing challenge of new frontiers of communication.

However, Smolla has collected a brief list of nine elements that modern American defamation law reflects (to varying degrees).

Paraphrased, they are:

- a claim is made (by a person/entity)
- that is false
- and defamatory
- concerning a wronged party (person/entity)
- that is somehow transmitted to a third-party (someone other than the one making the claims or being wronged)
- that is not secret or legally protected
- that causes some injury (whether actual or presumed)
- that is the result of a fault by the person making the claim
- that causes monetary harm in addition to reputational injury[6]

Even this list, which, in a perfect world, could be far more straightforward, has several qualifications that would have to be added to account for many jurisdictions and circumstances. This makes defamation cases complex and nearly impossible to discuss in a general sense. Every week, my webmaster receives submissions from people asking if they have been defamed, what they should do, and if they have any recourse. He has often asked, "Is there a general answer to these?" Sadly, there is not. Nearly every case must be treated differently. Much of this concerns how jurisdictions deal with the nine elements listed above.

Fortunately, there are a few general principles that can be applied safely. The foremost of these is, "Was the statement true?" In nearly every jurisdiction, the truth can be used as a valid defense for liability. You are usually safe if it is accurate and can be proven. In a few rare cases, for example, in Illinois, you must have good motives and a justifiable reason for stating the truth. But generally speaking, everyone is safer when confining themselves to things that can be proven true. Echoing the famous Ninth Commandment, "You shall not bear false witness against your neighbor," the world generally works better when we represent people accurately.

Another general principle is that the wronged party will usually have to demonstrate that they have been damaged somehow. This can take many forms, including financial, reputational, and emotional damage. Each category has different challenges when attempting to prove and estimate a monetary amount, but they are all effectively on the table.

Sadly, emotional distress, which is one of the most significant forms of damage a person can encounter, can sometimes be the most difficult to prove. But we now live in a world where the Internet has made nearly everyone a worldwide publisher. This means that when someone is defamed, it is effectively global. This causes the psychological harm victims receive to become staggering. I have witnessed this firsthand with my clients and have even experienced it myself.

Finally, another general takeaway is that we should all be cautious about what we say, write, and post online about others. Unless you know what you are saying is true or speaking under some form of legally privileged communication (for example, your priest, doctor, attorney, or spouse), it is best to keep it to yourself. There are, of course, provisions for political speech, opinion, and First Amendment rights, but when speaking about the people in our physical and online communities, we should be cautious. Will Rogers was famous for saying, "Never miss a good chance to shut up." This advice seems even more relevant in today's fast-moving digital age.

The Role of Personal Opinion & Freedom of Expression

Before Hillary Clinton became senator of New York, Daniel Patrick Moynihan occupied her seat for 24 years. This former advisor to Richard Nixon and ambassador to India has been quoted as saying, "You are entitled to your own opinion. But you are not entitled to your own facts." This sentiment is indelibly woven into the fabric of what it means to be an American. As Americans, we have opinions, and we are famous for wanting to express them boldly and loudly. We see it as our constitutional right under the First Amendment.

The court has upheld this, often with rather entertaining rulings. One of the more hilarious is Judge Welch's from the Massachusetts Superior Court. When ruling on *Knight v. Ryan*, his undertones and borderline sarcastic wit are unmistakable:

> In this country, everyone is entitled to his or her opinion no matter how ill-informed. And any opinionated soul can voice that opinion without fear of liability. While this permits an airing of many ridiculous and mean-spirited opinions, the alternative would be much worse. It is the freedom of speech guarantee enshrined in both the United States and Massachusetts constitutions that protects this free marketplace of ideas.

> ... if a well-known evangelist voices the opinion that Arial Sharon has angered God and thus suffered a stroke, that statement also is not actionable. No matter how ridiculous the opinion may be, it is entitled to a place in the free marketplace of ideas and is to be tested there for its validity.[7]

So, you might immediately ask yourself, *Well, how does this work with everything we previously said about defamation?* As with everything on this topic, the answer is complicated, and very smart people have struggled to answer it for a long time. I will spare you from a laborious review of the case history, the many ways the law has changed over the years, and the thousands of pages of analysis that have tried to answer this question. Of all the many turns and twists in defamation law, this is the most complicated and challenging to deal with. By establishing the First Amendment, our Founding Fathers set the right of free speech, but they made the defamation law far more complex.

On its face, the difference between a fact and an opinion is easy to understand. Facts are statements that can be proven true or false; they are objective and represent concrete realities. They might include things like, "Cats are mammals." Facts tend to be universally accepted truths based on evidence and verification. Conversely, opinions express a belief, attitude, value judgment, or how we feel about something.

An example would be, "Cats are the best animal ever to exist." They are subjective interpretations that cannot be proven or verified.[8] These concepts are taught early in our education and appear to be understood by most of the public. Using the example given above by Judge Welch, nobody can prove that God was angry at Ariel Sharon. The statement cannot be falsified as, at least to date, no one can prove God's opinion about modern politics (or even sports). Indeed, the issue of whether something is verifiable or falsifiable is critical to legal determinations.

So, what is the problem? Why is it so complex? Issues arise for several different reasons. First and foremost, it can be difficult to define when someone is engaging in defamatory speech or just expressing their opinion. Second, differing standards apply in an attempt to keep an open marketplace of ideas. We will look at some of these details in the following sections.

Hyperbolic Language: Claim Nobody Takes You Seriously

The more hyperbolic the language, the less likely the listeners will understand it as "fact." Daniel Novack and Sara Shyabian noted this rise in the modern era with their guest column, published in the *Hollywood Reporter* in 2021, where they used the term "libel-proof defendant." Historically, the term "libel-proof plaintiff" has been used in defamation cases to describe someone with no reputation to protect.[9] That is someone who, for one reason or another, has no "good name" that can be besmirched and, therefore, cannot claim to have a reputation that has been injured.

The libel-proof defendant, by contrast, has a public image so rooted in hyperbole, political discourse, or entertainment that nothing they say can be taken seriously. It brings to mind the defense employed by John Stewart in his 2004 interview on the CNN show *Crossfire*. In this famous 15-minute segment, Stewart lambasted Tucker Carlson (and journalism) for trying to hold him to some form of journalistic integrity and accusing him of partisan hackery.

Stewart's famous response still echoes to this day. "You are on CNN. The show that leads into me is puppets making crank phone calls. What is wrong with you?... You have a responsibility to public discourse."[10] With this interview, whether knowingly or not, Stewart formed the core of an argument about rhetoric and believability. Who could take the opinions and news reporting seriously of a man on a network known for comedy whose program is preceded by the show *Crank Yankers*, featuring puppet re-enactments of celebrity phone calls?

There is still a rigorous internet debate about whether this episode led to the cancellation of *Crossfire* and the firing of Tucker Carlson from CNN. Carlson claims that he was already on the way out of CNN. But, it is interesting to note that years later, when the Fox News Network was faced with a defamation case aimed at *Tucker Carlson Tonight* by former Playboy model Karen McDougal, the issue of rhetorical hyperbole and opinion once again came to the forefront.[11]

Echoing the "Stewart Defense," Fox's lawyers claimed that Tucker's viewers tuned in for precisely this type of "overheated rhetoric" to promote debate for the overall public concern. That is, nobody was treating it as a news fact. It did not matter if Tucker believed the details were accurate or if he said on his show, "Remember the facts of the story. These are undisputed." Nobody, claimed the lawyers, tuned in to the show expecting to hear the truth.[12] When dismissing the case, the judge agreed with this assessment. Fox was not alone in successfully using this defense, nor was it particularly new. However, with the rise of bombastic personalities who command a loyal and sometimes near-rabid audience, this defense has taken center stage in the defamation debate. The legal standard is often referenced as "what a reasonable person might believe." Whether or not the vast majority of podcast followers represent a judge's standard of reasonableness and what this means for the law have yet to be determined.

Who Decides What is True?

As Americans, we value a vibrant marketplace of ideas. So much so that we must actively protect it by maintaining a strict code that upholds the highest standards and practices. The proper remedy to lousy information is better information, not suppression. Rather than suppress ideas, we have historically trusted each other to sift through the weeds and make a good evaluation. While this has been tested in recent years, it still holds. We may have conquered the frontier and "Wild West," taming it with civilization and industry, but the marketplace of ideas remains as wild as any West we have ever won.

So, who decides what is accurate, and what rules govern the difference between fact and opinion? To date, I am unaware of anyone who has been able to put forth a consistent and universal standard on this issue, and it does not look like we are anywhere close to creating one. Instead, when looking at case law, it would appear that "niches" have formed around various topics, almost like the cliques we dreaded in high school. Each one has its own set of rules and standards of behavior. We all learned that the social rules were different for the jocks, the band geeks, the cool kids, and the nerds. You had to know which group was governing at any given moment, heed their social norms, and avoid the ones you could not comply with. Depending on what time of history we are living in, each of these niches ranges from reasonably harmless to outright dangerous.

Some portions of society are driven by subjective opinions or ideas that cannot be falsified. Take, for example, restaurant reviews. A simple Google search on "defamation cases about bad reviews" will send you into a deep rabbit hole. While I cannot find specific statistics, the activity around legal action (threatened and actual) regarding bad reviews is overwhelming. But historically, it has seemed rare that any restaurant or business can be successful in such a case. A reviewer would have to move into precise details far outside the level of opinion to come close to liability, and even then, they would likely be protected.

Online reviewers have figured this out and have wielded their power en masse. In 2022, *Mashed.com* reported a story about a restaurant bombed with negative reviews because an employee claimed they had not been paid.[13] Online activists (without the appearance of reviewing the story's validity) took to inundating the establishment with bad reviews as punishment. While there are processes for businesses to respond to reviews or eventually remove them, the implications can be intimidating. I have seen a restaurant run out of business by knowingly false statements that gained traction on social media, leading to a boycott. By the time the lies were exposed it was too late, and investors lost their money.

While the previous example may seem relatively harmless to society (although undoubtedly crucial to the individual business owner), other niches have far more dire consequences. This was displayed globally and in real-time during the 2020 COVID-19 pandemic. Infection cases and death data were made readily available to the public for immediate analysis by anyone who could download it, and the news cycle was ever-evolving as we all learned more together. This created one of the most significant medical, psychological, academic, and scientific disputes ever. My team and I saw countless examples of personal, professional, and religious relationships break down as everyone tried to figure out the truth. Everyone had an authority figure they followed on social media, television, or radio—the "trusted voice" that gave them an accurate read on the situation.

The rise of "independent fact-checkers" came to the forefront of the informational madness that ensued. These supposed independent arbiters of truth claimed to have no agenda other than reporting what was faithful to the public and reining in the evils of "disinformation." While the idea sounds noble (and fact-checking websites have been helpful since the Internet was founded), scientific and academic truth does not always reveal itself on our timetable. The simple fact was that we were, and still are, learning what happened, what is true about COVID and the vaccine, and the overall impact on our world. This is not due to conspiracies or agendas, but because experimentation takes time and iteration.

Sadly, during the COVID pandemic, the same dynamics were at play as with the restaurant reviews. If the majority opinion moved in a particular direction, and they could get enough articles and assessments out there to establish "fact," then anyone outside that majority opinion could be "fact-checked," labeled, or even deplatformed for repeated violations of what was deemed misinformation. In a later chapter of this book, we will look at the case where I had the privilege of serving as counsel to Candace Owens in her suit against some of these fact-checkers and their censoring of her for even quoting medical opinions by a doctor who had a dissenting view of the developing COVID pandemic.

Digging Out of the Mud

There is much more to be discussed regarding the nuances around which defamation laws orbit. My intention in covering the above particulars that must be considered when evaluating whether a person has been defamed, is to help us understand that there is a war waging around how words are used. It is subtle, and it is often silent. Many of the people or organizations engaging in this war have an army of legal soldiers who help them craft their words in ways that cause confusion, undermine their opponents, obfuscate important (and possibly opinion-impacting) information—the list goes on and on. What is the prize in this battle? Increased influence, higher dollars, fame. Ultimately, the prize is power.

It is easy to read examples of entertainers like John Stewart or politicians, and think that this is only a battle being fought in arenas outside of the daily concern of the common person. This is not the case. As we will see, it is regular citizens (like Nick Sandmann and many others) who become cannon fodder in this battle for power and influence. Incidents that would normally barely be blips on the radar between ordinary people are being videoed, edited, posted, editorialized, and broadcast almost instantly—all framed to serve the agendas of those trying to control a narrative.

Sadly, when the dust settles and those same ordinary folks try to recover their reputation by holding those who wrongly mischaracterized them to account, they are all too often stopped in their tracks by poorly understood and outdated laws or worse, judges that pay more attention to which side of the political divide will benefit (or suffer) depending on their ruling.

Chapter Notes

1 Kentucky Distillers' Association, "Kentucky Bourbon Trail Trip Planner," 2024, accessed May 24, 2024, https://kybourbontrail.com/itineraries/kentucky-bourbon-trail/.

2 Merriam-Webster.com, "Definition of Defamation," Merriam Webster, last modified 14 May 2024, accessed May 24, 2024, https://www.merriam-webster.com/dictionary/defamation.

3 Rodney A. Smolla, Law of Defamation, Second Edition ed., 2 vols. (Eagan, MN: Thomson Reuters, 1999).

4 Smolla.

5 Smolla.

6 Smolla.

7 Knight v. Ryan, 2006 WL 307974 (Mass. Super. Ct. 2206)

8 "Understanding the Difference between Fact and Opinion," Financial Crime Academy, May 24, 20242024, https://financialcrimeacademy.org/difference-between-fact-and-opinion/.

9 Daniel Novak, and Sara Shayanian, "Rhetorical Hyperbole Is the Defamation Defense Du Jour (Guest Column)," last modified April 14, 2021, 2021, accessed May 24, 2024, https://www.hollywoodreporter.com/business/business-news/rhetorical-hyperbole-is-the-defamation-defense-du-jour-guest-column-4166328/.

10 Crossfire, CNN, 2004.; "Jon Stewart Tangles with Cnn's crossfire," 2004, accessed May 24, 2024, https://bradt.ca/blog/jon-stewart-tangles-with-cnn-crossfire/.

11 McDougal v. Fox News Network, LLC, No. 1:2019cv11161 - Document 39 (S.D.N.Y. 2020)

12 Elpidio Valdes, "Fox News: State Television and Propaganda," last modified Apr 29, 2022, 2022, accessed May 24, 2024, https://elpidio.org/2022/04/29/fox-news-state-television-and-propaganda/.

13 Ree Winter, "The Accusation That Had Tiktok Spamming a Restaurant with Bad Reviews," last modified July 8, 2022, 2022, accessed May 24, 2024, https://www.mashed.com/921822/the-accusation-that-had-tiktok-spamming-a-restaurant-with-bad-reviews/.

NOBODY IS SAFE

DEFAMATION'S IMPACT ON THE CITIZEN

"It is easier to build strong children than to repair broken men."
- Frederick Douglass

Throughout this book, we discuss the facts and law surrounding Nick Sandmann's case. For right now, let's focus on his age. He was 16 when the media mob attacked him. The main thing that hit me way back in January 2019, when all of this happened, was just how incredibly irresponsible the press was in allowing the publication of news stories and articles about a kid! Really?

The fact that the corporate media, which is historically liberal, attacked a kid left me speechless. But that has proven to be a naïve reaction. In 2019, I was just starting my career in defamation law. I had so much more to learn.

In this chapter, we will apply some of my learning about hit pieces to another more recent case, where an unhinged "woke" reporter aimed his keyboard at a kid even younger than Nick Sandmann. On November 26, 2023, *Deadspin*,[1] a sports website that brings you "Sports News Without Fear, Favor or Compromise" (ha ha), published an article attacking a nine-year-old boy whom we will refer to as H.A. This young boy was attending a Kansas City Chiefs' game. You may recall this game because H.A. was wearing an elaborate Native American headdress and had on face paint, half black and half red. Chiefs fans routinely wear black and red face paint. While I was not the least bit surprised by the attack, I still thought to myself when I first read about it, "Again?"

The article published by Deadspin and written by Carron J. Phillips was titled *The NFL needs to speak out against the Kansas City Chiefs fan in Black face, Native headdress*. The article pictured nine-year-old H.A., but it only showed the right side of his face—the side that was painted black. This fact is the key piece of evidence that not only empowered the effort to cancel H.A. but was also the tactic his lawyers used to come to his defense. By showing only the black side of his face and headdress, the author set up young H.A. to be racist on two fronts; showing disrespect to both Black people and Native Americans.

As outlined in the Complaint filed by his lawyers at Clare Locke LLP[2], the camera found H.A. in the stands proudly wearing his Chiefs' attire. He stared intently at the field, and the fact that he (like a few hundred other fans) had his face painted half black and half red, was evident. The picture also shows a young boy who appears to be white.

According to his LinkedIn profile, the so-called journalist who authored this article earned his Bachelor of Arts in 2006 from Morehouse College, majoring in African American/ Black Studies.[3] While Morehouse College does not list Mr. Phillips' major, its Division of Humanities has quite a lot to say about social justice. So, I assume Mr. Phillips went to this historically Black college and was steeped in the teaching of social justice.

H.A.'s Complaint goes into detail about Mr. Phillips' journalism career, and focuses on multiple divisive race-based articles he wrote.[4] According to the Complaint, Mr. Phillips presented the story as a person who sees life through a racial lens, always focusing on what's wrong regarding race versus what is right.

Before jumping into the expertly crafted lawsuit, let's consider why Deadspin decided to attack a nine-year-old boy, presumably white, for being a racist. The main reason is that H.A. was *assumed* to be a white boy (ironically, he is a Native American), who could be easily framed to appear to be a double racist. As we will carefully analyze later, hit jobs are executed in a scripted fashion. There are three distinct steps: (1) an oversimplified presentation, (2) emotional puppet mastering, and (3) looking strong, acting weak.

The Deadspin article followed this script to the letter. It showed an incomplete and edited photo of a kid in an Indian headdress—a shockingly oversimplified presentation. By showing only the black side of his face, the picture of H.A. was designed to create an emotional reaction from the viewer.

I will confess that when I first saw it, even as a veteran of the culture war, I was momentarily shocked. However, after taking thirty seconds to ponder, I immediately saw the hit job in process. Deadspin was not just attacking a nine-year-old; it was fighting the racist NFL. In its mind, it was only doing "God's work." Mr. Phillips made it his business to show that the NFL was the real target, not young H.A., who was only the means to attack the NFL.

I don't buy this at all. I have fielded hundreds of calls from families, athletes, academics, professionals, executives, nurses, high school students, doctors, lawyers, accountants, salesman—virtually any profession. Every one of these calls was in response to a cancellation effort based upon one of three things. The first is being white. The second is being a Christian. The third is anything to do with DEI and LGBTQIA+ issues. So, being a straight white Christian is a very dangerous mix.

The main thing I hear from people who call is that they are not a racist, a transphobe, an Islamophobe, or opposed to equality in the workplace. So many of these people are in abject fear of being disliked, and just cannot believe that they are being culled from the herd. Sadly, who you are does not matter. Instead, it is who they make you. So, when Mr. Phillips saw this *white* boy, whom he could make into a double racist, he seized the moment.

Of course, he also stepped into a huge pile of dung when it turned out his "easy target" was a Native American, whose father and grandfather were both strongly associated with their Native American Tribe. This truth, along with significant social media backlash, turned Mr. Phillips' story from an attack piece into a self-inflicted wound. The fact that H.A. was an actual Native American took the sword of cultural appropriation from the hand of the accusers, and reduced the mob attacking H.A. by half.

With the mob reduced, the attack fizzled. Deadspin and Mr. Phillips then came under attack. Personally, I think had H.A. not been a Native American, the attack against him would have been worse. There would have been two transgressions instead of one to talk about. The stage was set. The hit job was launched but was quickly undone when young H.A. was found *not* to be the white villain hoped for.

So, what happened next? Well, H.A.'s parents did the smart thing and reached out to one of the premier plaintiff's defamation law firms in the country, Clare Locke LLP. I have had the pleasure of meeting Tom Clare and Libby Locke, the husband-and-wife co-founders of the law firm. Tom and Libby started their careers with a much larger national law firm, but left to found their own boutique law firm dedicated to representing plaintiffs in defamation matters.

According to its website, the firm focuses on pre-publication counseling, post-publication retractions, and defamation litigation.[5] This is exactly what I do, and it can be quite interesting work.

The Key Elements of a Defamation Suit

Let us quickly review what these key elements of a defamation law practice mean to a defamation lawsuit. Many cases do not just pop up like the Deadspin case. Instead, some start when a person receives a call from a reporter or school administrator who has a question. The typical question involves some transgression of DEI, LGBTQIA+, or religious issues.

A classic question is to explain something like why your reference to Islam in your Sunday sermon was perceived by some to be racist. Or, explain why you were seen wearing a Trump 2020 hat on the campus commons. Or one of your teammates heard you make what they thought to be a homophobic comment to a person on your soccer team.

These questions are uniformly based on race, religion, or culture (LGBTQIA+/DEI). Much of the work involved in defending yourself from defamation often occurs prior to publication. If you are able to engage before anything is published, any lawyers familiar with defamation will offer some pre-publication counseling. In short, pre-publication counseling involves a series of letters and phone calls threatening a lawsuit if the reporter, manager, or school administrator makes public the false and defamatory allegation. Sometimes, if the allegation is true, pre-publication counseling involves a plea not to end a person's job or academic career over the mistake.

I am often contacted by a client (or their legal counsel) and asked to provide pre-publication counseling. Most lawyers do not regularly deal with defamation cases, and when they suddenly find themselves in the crosshairs of a potential defamation firestorm, I will be brought onto their team to provide an assist.

In one such case, I acquired a client whose work was nationally recognized on several social issues. He had been approached by a reporter who was preparing a story, one that obviously implied that my client was a racist. Despite the facts of the situation, which totally disproved the foundation of the reporter's question, he was going to press ahead with the story. Fortunately, I had been brought into the situation early.

Armed with the truth about the client and their views, I obtained all the legal approvals required and contacted the editor of the national news organization that was about to publish the false and defamatory story. Taking a firm position with the editor, I requested that he hold off with the story until I could provide more detail. He did so.

Through continued negotiations, I demonstrated to the editor why the publication was false and defamatory. Not wanting to budge, the editor argued that the publication was based on provable facts, and the reporter's opinion about those facts.

When you get to the point where you are going back and forth with an editor, the story will usually end up being run. But the purpose is not simply to stop them from publishing; it is to be able to show that the news organization published the story despite strong evidence to the contrary. This dramatically increases their liability in future litigation.

Fortunately, in this case, the strategy worked. This was because the publication had spent a lot of time reporting on this nationally known matter, and as I warned them, the lawsuit would expose the false premise underlying the news publication's narrative on the topic.

Ultimately, the news organization decided to leave my client alone for fear a lawsuit might distract from the false premise it had established when reporting on the subject. It continued to elaborate on the false narrative it had spent so much time creating.

The next phase of the defamation lawsuit is the demand for a post-publication retraction. Many states have laws that require a party injured by defamation to first ask the entity that published the defamatory comment to retract it and apologize. This should involve a publication just as conspicuous as the defamatory publication that tells the readers the author was wrong, and sets the record straight. In a just and polite society, an apology for being wrong would also help.

A demand for retraction is normally a prerequisite even when not required by statute. Suppose the potential plaintiff does not first ask for a retraction, often within a limited period of time. In that case, the plaintiff may not be able to pursue punitive damages (in states that do not require a plaintiff to issue a retraction demand, case law often states that a failure to retract can subject the defendant to punitive damages). The logic is that when a publication is told that it is wrong, the defamatory statement should be retracted. But when it refuses, the defendant risks a jury instruction on punitive damages because it had a chance to correct the record, but instead doubled down.

As outlined throughout this book, the law of defamation is so favorable to the press and others that defame people, that the threat of punitive damages is almost quaint. The reality is that very smart lawyers have to exercise all of their brain cells to fashion a theory of liability that is not stymied by the existing law. Stick with this book, and you will understand why I say this.

Applying This to the Deadspin Case

So, what did H.A. do? Let me share what his lawyers alleged in the Complaint. They first tried to persuade Deadspin to retract (spoiler alert, it did not). As outlined in the Complaint, H.A.'s lawyers sent a retraction demand to Deadspin demanding it retract and apologize. Deadspin refused—choosing instead to issue an Editor's Note explaining that its reporting about H.A. was "unfortunate," and its intent was to focus on the NFL and its checkered history on race.[6]

Admitting you screwed up and missed your target, but then refusing to take down the offending article or apologize, is a recipe for disaster. But the brain trust at Deadspin felt differently. It chose to stick by its "journalistic ethics" and defend the "integrity of the press." Deadspin treated H.A. as just an unfortunate casualty in the quest to criticize the racist NFL.

As outlined in H.A.'s Complaint, Deadspin continued to scramble to avoid the likely catastrophic consequences of its reporting. It changed the gist of its report from a racist kid to "every stadium in the [NFL] league" should ban Indian headdresses. I really wonder if Deadspin had called in its lawyers by this point, because instead of improving the situation, it was making things worse. To attempt to turn the narrative from *We trashed a little kid* to *We were really just attacking the racist NFL and sorry you misunderstood* did not do anything to reduce Deadspin's liability. Worse, it did nothing to address the reporter's incompetence and Deadspin's tone-deaf response.

On the issue of incompetence and tone-deafness, I would be remiss not to point out the obvious conclusion that Deadspin and its reporter sincerely believed that they were right. Mr. Phillips is likely steeped in social justice teachings, and despite being a highly educated man privileged to write about sports on a national platform, he feels oppressed rather than grateful. Objectively, that view strikes many of us as irrational and false. But without dipping into philosophy, this is how revolutions begin. One side believes it is absolutely right. So does the other. The correct view, in my opinion, is that children and private individuals should be left alone to live their lives. But, people like Phillips do not even consider the very real damage done to H.A. and his parents.

Before we move on to the next step in analyzing a defamation lawsuit, the case involving H.A. seems an appropriate point for me to share my thoughts about why the press attacks kids. In my years in the defamation arena, I have encountered many other children who have been attacked by the media. Based on these experiences and other attacks on minors by school administrators and coaches, the conclusion seems obvious: those who seek to impose their radical Progressive and social justice agendas often go after the most vulnerable in our society.

All reasonable people are horrified when a kid is singled out for attack. And most people are too afraid (or vulnerable themselves) to stand in the gap. The spectacle of attacking a child is so frightening that those observing the attack will self-censor and silence themselves out of fear.

Moving on, the next phase of the defamation lawsuit is the actual Complaint, which is filed in court against the defendant. In this case, H.A., through his parents, sued Deadspin. Before the suit is filed, the lawyers must carefully consider the facts and defenses available to the newspaper. Many defamation lawsuits are dismissed in the early stages based upon decisions a judge, not a jury, makes. Judges are the gatekeepers tasked to protect newspapers from lawsuits. Presumably, this is to protect the press's freedoms and free expression. Practically speaking, the lawful protections afforded to the press allow them to engage in cancellations (like the one inflicted on H.A.) without fear of legal reprisals.

The first decision to be made is *whom* to sue. In H.A.'s Complaint, his lawyers sued the company that owns Deadspin. It named, but did not sue, the reporter, Mr. Phillips. I am not certain why they did not sue the reporter, but my best guess is that to have sued the reporter might have made it more difficult to sue Deadspin in the state of Delaware. Choosing *where* to sue is the next important decision. About two-thirds of the states have anti-SLAPP laws. SLAPP stands for Strategic Lawsuit Against Public Participation. We discuss anti-SLAPP laws in more detail later, as they are one of the most potent defenses the media uses to scare plaintiffs into not suing for defamation. These laws, and others like them, drive the calculus behind *where* to sue.

Once a location has been chosen, the next step is to draft a complaint that anticipates the potential defenses the media will raise through a *motion to dismiss* (this is typically filed at the very beginning of the lawsuit). A motion to dismiss contends that the plaintiff has not stated sufficient facts to sustain his claim. So, what must a defamation plaintiff set out in his complaint to be successful? Here is a brief outline of the elements.

To be actionable as defamation, a publication must contain false statements. These false statements must constitute statements of fact, not opinion, and must be published. Finally, actionable statements must have been uttered with the requisite state of mind/intent—this is *negligence* in the case of private plaintiffs, and *actual malice* for plaintiffs who are public figures. H.A. is not a public figure, so he needs to allege only negligence. To be negligent for an action, the defendant must have had a duty to act with reasonable care, and have then breached that duty, causing the plaintiff injury.

As stated above, Deadspin's failure to investigate this story at all breached the duties outlined by *The Society of Professional Journalists Code of Ethics*, which requires a reporter to take greater care when reporting about private individuals, especially when they are children.[7]

The central tenant of defamation law is the publication of false statements that *appear* true. Here, the assertion that H.A. was wearing "blackface," which is generally considered racist, was a false fact. A statement of fact is provably or verifiably true or false. It cannot constitute an opinion. Opinion includes political commentary, consumer views, policy statements, satire, humor, editorials, and the like. However, even a statement that appears to be an opinion may imply or suggest underlying facts that are themselves actionable as defamation.

This tenant is applicable to H.A.—and his lawyers said as much. While Deadspin will claim that calling H.A. a racist was just an opinion, in his Complaint, H.A.'s lawyers pointed out that Deadspin showed only one side of his face by picking out one second of a video of H.A.In essence, this concealed that he was dressing like many other Kansas City Chiefs fans, wearing both black and red. This concealment was a decision designed to allow the reporter to frame a narrative of "racist white children." In addition, Deadspin's article also suggested it possessed underlying facts about H.A.'s parents, when Deadspin stated H.A.'s parents taught him "racism and hate" in the home.

The next consideration in crafting a defamation complaint is whether the false statements are actually defamatory. Deadspin could have criticized H.A. for his face paint color choices, saying he should have used the official red Pantone color of the Chiefs (PMS 186 C). That would not have been defamatory; it would have been humorous. To be actionable, the false statements of fact must be defamatory in character. To be defamatory, a statement must bring the plaintiff into disrepute, obloquy (a legal term for disgrace), or otherwise harm the plaintiff's reputation.

Statements that tend to lower a person in the estimation of the community, or deter third persons from associating or dealing with him, are usually considered defamatory. As factually stated in H.A.'s Complaint, both he and his parents have been shunned and avoided in their community to such a degree that the family is considering relocating.

Some false statements are damaging with only the words of the statement. These statements are *defamatory per se*. Per se means "by itself." Defamatory per se statements are so obviously degrading or pernicious that no consideration of context or proof of reputational harm is required. In my opinion, to state that H.A. "found a way to hate Black people and Native Americans at the same time" by painting the team's colors on his face and wearing a headdress like many other fans is obviously defamatory per se.

We know Deadspin published these defamatory per se comments, but is it liable? This is the next consideration in drafting a defamation lawsuit. To be liable for defamation, the defendant must have uttered a false and defamatory statement of fact with a malicious intention. For H.A., who is a private figure, his lawyers need to prove only that Deadspin was negligent in publishing the defamatory statement. Failure to take reasonable care to determine the truth is sufficient for H.A.'s case.

The types of people defamation law refers to as *public figures* tend to bring many defamation lawsuits, but they face a higher bar to hold the media liable. Public figures must prove that what was written about them was done with *actual malice*. Actual malice means that the defendant knew that what he was about to say was false, but decided to publish it anyway out of malicious intent or with reckless disregard for the effects of his statement. Public figures include celebrities or politicians, who are known by name by many people.

So, what will Deadspin do in response to H.A.'s complaint that spells out, in a factual manner, what Deadspin did? Here is a rundown of what the press usually says. The primary defense it could use is that what it published was the truth. Truth is an absolute defense to defamation. In other words, even if statements made are factual, defamatory, and damaging—if the statements are true, the plaintiff has no case. If you actually served time in jail for murder, to call you a murderer is not defamatory—it is true.

The next defense Deadspin will raise is that its reporting is merely its opinion based upon what it observed. It will say it saw H.A. and interpreted his face paint and headdress to be an assault on Black people and Native Americans. H.A. preemptively responded to this in his Complaint, arguing that to call his face paint "blackface" was a statement of fact and not opinion. Unfortunately, this determination is what lawyers call a *question of law* and is decided at the outset by the judge.

So, H.A.'s judge could easily dismiss the lawsuit against Deadspin by deciding that Deadspin's statements were merely its opinion based upon what it observed. The *opinion defense* (which is an *absolute defense*) is a major barrier to defamation lawsuits because a judge, not a jury, makes this call. So, if the judge is a champion of a free press, he might be more inclined to give the press a pass.

Assuming H.A.'s case survives a motion to dismiss, and I think it will, what might he recover from Deadspin? I suspect his damages will be significant. The primary form of defamation damages is called *presumed damages*. This form of defamation damages is premised on the idea that once you have been defamed, it is impossible to know what people really think about you, because if they think you are a "double racist," they will not tell you. Instead, for a child, other children and parents might not invite him for a cookout or birthday party. He will be shunned, but not know exactly by whom. He will only know that he has few friends he can really trust. So, a jury is allowed to state what damages it presumes he suffered because it is impossible to prove why no one invited him to their high school graduation party. Presumed damages get to the heart of reputational harm—he has been cast out of polite society, and that hurts.

H.A. will also be able to pursue significant damages for his actual losses, which include things like future lost wages, past and future medical treatment, and emotional distress. When a person is publicly canceled as H.A. was, he suffers a lifetime of damages often referred to as *perpetual reputational harm* (I talk about this in a later chapter). You could also call them *forever damages*, because you will be able to search H.A. online for the rest of his life, and the incident will still be there. If you don't believe me, just search *Duke lacrosse case.*

These damages will also be quite significant. As H.A.'s lawyers stated in the Complaint, for the rest of his life, potential employers will look up H.A. and discover that the intelligent and clever young man sitting across the table from them was accused of being a double racist. This could be just enough for the employer to choose the other job applicant over H.A. All of this is quite intimidating.

Finally, H.A. has also asked for an award of *punitive damages*, which are available in defamation actions if the plaintiff can prove the defendant acted with willful, malicious intent.

You now know quite a bit about H.A.'s case—so you can decide for yourself. My vote is for a hefty award of punitive damages sufficient to put Deadspin and its owner out of business. This will send the right message.

So, What's Next?

Where does H.A.'s case go from here? Assuming H.A. survives the coming motion to dismiss (based upon Deadspin's argument that it reported the truth, or what it wrote was protected opinion), H.A.'s case will move into what lawyers call *discovery*. This is the phase of the case where each side is allowed to ask the other for documents to prove its case. H.A. will ask for all of Deadspin's internal communications about the article, such as text messages and emails. In addition, H.A. will ask for the video Deadspin edited to prove that Deadspin knew it was concealing the truth when it showed only the right side of his face.

Then, H.A.'s lawyers will take the depositions of the reporter, the editor, the person who edited the video, and others who can shed light on exactly how the story was written and published. The goal will be to prove that Deadspin was negligent in its failure to investigate the facts of the article. Had Deadspin just picked up the phone, it would have immediately learned that H.A. was a Native American. That would have killed the story on the spot. But Deadspin could only see a white boy, and because of its own bias, it never considered there might be a different reality.

After H.A.'s lawyers conduct discovery, there will be another effort to dismiss the case in a process called a *motion for summary judgment*. A motion is simply a written document that asks a court to take a particular action. A motion for summary judgment asks the court to dismiss the case upon consideration of all of the facts developed in the discovery phase. In general, motions for summary judgment are not favored by courts. Usually, if there is a dispute about a material fact, a court should defer to the ruling of a jury of peers. In my experience, it is always better to let a jury decide, because they will more closely represent the interests of the community. The more decision-makers that are involved, the more individual bias is filtered out.

Assuming the court does not grant summary judgment, the case will go to trial. As it approaches trial, both sides carefully consider the pros and cons of a trial. Often, defendants want to avoid a nuclear verdict and settle before the case goes to trial. This causes the plaintiffs to decide if a settlement is in the best interest of H.A. Lawyers then have the ethical duty to do what is best for their clients. Often, a multimillion-dollar settlement that could set H.A. up for life is better than the risk of a trial. But H.A. and his family may decide they want to teach Deadspin and the media a lesson. So, they may decide on a trial. I hope that is what they do.

In conclusion, these are the considerations and stages of how an actual defamation case is put together and brought to trial. The value of the time involved in a case like H.A.'s can run well into seven figures. It is an intense, time-consuming, and challenging undertaking. I commend H.A., his family, and their lawyers for going after Deadspin in the pursuit of justice.

Chapter Notes

---

[1] For purposes of readability, the author has chosen not to italicize the proper name "Deadspin" for the remainder of the chapter.

2 Armenta v. G/O Media Inc. (Del. Super. Ct.)

3 Lance Fernandez, "Who Is Carron J. Phillips? Deadspin Writer under Fire for Accusing Chiefs Fan of Blackface and Racism," last modified Nov 29, 2023, 2023, accessed May 24, 2024, https://www.msn.com/en-us/sports/nfl/who-is-carron-j-phillips-deadspin-writer-under-fire-for-accusing-chiefs-fan-of-blackface-and-racism/ar-AA1kIhxe.

4 Fernandez

5 "Clare Locke Llp," 2024, accessed May 24, 2024, https://clarelocke.com/.

6 Carron J. Phillips, "The Nfl Must Ban Native Headdress and Culturally Insensitive Face Paint in the Stands (Updated)," 2023, accessed May 24, 2024, https://deadspin.com/roger-goodell-kansas-city-chiefs-fan-black-face-native-1851048905/.

7 Society of Professional Journalists, "Code of Ethics," (2014), https://www.spj.org/pdf/spj-code-of-ethics.pdf.

FACT AND OPINION

THE TRUTH WILL SET YOU FREE? DON'T BE SO NAIVE

"People often claim to hunger for truth,
but seldom like the taste when it's served up."
- George R.R. Martin

The truth, the whole truth, and nothing but the truth. Every courtroom drama inevitably has a scene with a witness taking the stand, placing their hand on a Bible, and repeating that phrase, promising they will be honest, forthright, and complete in their courtroom testimony. Truth, rightly so, has held a central place in virtually every society as far back as we can track. Without truth, anything goes.

But what do we do when truth and opinion mix? Or worse, when truth and opinion mix and certain portions of the truth (usually the portions of truth that stand in opposition to the opinion being expressed) are left out? Sadly, even though we live in an era where virtually every moment is captured on camera when it comes to people experiencing defamation, trimming truth and stitching it together with salacious opinion has become the norm. And why not? A truncated video or audio clip, framed with false exposition, can often be more compelling to an unwitting audience than the same false exposition without anything to accompany it.

It's one thing to speak of this phenomenon in a philosophical manner. It's another to see it applied to a real-world situation. In Chapter one, I wrote about the evening that my wife and I learned of the altercation in which Nick Sandmann found himself back in 2019. With this question of truth as our backdrop, I'd like to examine a very specific timeline of what happened to Nick in Washington, D.C. We will look at the players involved, the actions taken, and the physical locations—all in an effort to establish a true picture of the events of that day. I'm not looking to relitigate this case. Instead, I want to use Nick's situation to help us better understand just how quickly a situation can be twisted into a narrative that can have far-reaching consequences for everyone involved.

Below is a recount of the now-familiar situation in which Nick Sandmann found himself back in 2019. In order to focus on just the facts, I've stripped away as much of the editorialization around intent, interpretation, or the post-news-cycle justification that ensued. While this may not be as titillating as we're used to reading, I think it is instructive for us to review it so that we can look at it through an even and measured lens:

The afternoon of January 18, 2019, was a busy one in Washington, D.C. The 46th annual March for Life, protesting the Supreme Court's ruling on *Roe vs. Wade*, making abortion legal in all 50 states, was wrapping up. Simultaneously, the Indigenous People's March, a gathering supporting the Dakota Access Pipeline protests, was being held.

As the March for Life was ending, a group of students from Covington Catholic High School in Covington, Kentucky, were waiting for their bus near the Lincoln Memorial. Participants in the Indigenous People's March were passing by the Memorial at the same time. In addition to these two groups, roughly five representatives from a group calling themselves Black Hebrew Israelites were milling about, yelling at passersby, and shouting "scriptures" from the red books they held.

For reasons many have only speculated about, the individuals from the Black Hebrew Israelites began to focus the majority of their shouts toward the students from Covington Catholic. The taunts were wide-ranging and insulting. From videos that were posted, as well as testimony from attendees, the phrases "you give faggots rights," "a bunch of incest babies," "dirty-ass little crackers," and "school shooters" were hurled at the Covington students—all coming from the members of the Black Hebrew Israelites.[1] However, the Black Hebrew Israelites did not focus solely on the Covington Catholic students. They could be heard telling members of the Indigenous People's March that the term "Indian means savage," calling them things like "buffalo worshipers," and using various racial slurs toward others while making their way past them.

In response to what was being shouted at them, students from Covington Catholic began to yell familiar chants that they would use at sporting events, and clap along to the drums coming from the Indigenous People's March. However, as the slurs became more intense, some of the students could be heard telling the members of the Black Hebrew Israelites to "cool it," "calm down," or simply reacting with "Woah!" The scene was escalating quickly.

As the high school students continued to chant and dance in response to the taunts from the Black Hebrew Israelites, Nathan Phillips, a drummer in the Indigenous People's March, interpreted their actions as disrespectful, so he and some of his group began making their way toward the students. Shortly afterward, Mr. Phillips came face-to-face with a young man named Nick Sandmann, who was wearing a red Make America Great Again hat. Mr. Sandmann stood in place as Mr. Phillips walked straight up to him, banging his drum and singing what was later described as an inter-tribal Native American song. Mr. Phillips got so close to Mr. Sandmann that his drum hit Mr. Sandmann's shirt collar at one point. For his part, Nick Sandmann said nothing. He stood still, a small smile on his face, holding eye contact with Mr. Phillips without moving an inch. During the face-to-face encounter, other students from Covington Catholic surrounded Nick and Mr. Phillips, continuing to clap, dance, and sing school spirit songs.

After approximately two minutes, Mr. Phillips and Mr. Sandmann parted ways—the encounter between The Indigenous People's March and the Covington Catholic students was over. There were no inflammatory words exchanged between Nick and Mr. Phillips. No tangential physical altercation occurred in the crowd surrounding them. No riot broke out. No one was hurt, and no property was damaged. As quickly as it started, it ended.

Why Did This Become Such a Big Deal?

Even now—having spent years representing Nick in court, talking on news programs, writing briefs and Op-Eds—when I review the facts of the case, I'm flabbergasted that this ever became headline news. Go to any sporting event across this great nation, and you're guaranteed to see or hear much worse than what happened on the steps of the Lincoln Memorial. To borrow from a prominent (but not very good) pundit—this event was a Nothing Burger. Even if it merits social or political analysis, if we focus on the truth of what happened, I am hard-pressed to understand how Nick came to be the person on which the media focused.

The other side of the coin, of course, is the possibility that I have a confirmation bias. After all, I have spent years fighting on Nick's side. Maybe I'm incapable of seeing some small yet important detail that implicates Nick and his classmates. Perhaps the media got it right. Maybe the events of that day should have not only been highlighted, but Nick should have been the one on which to place the blame.

In an effort to step outside of my own "echo chamber," I fed the above summary into an AI, asking it to review the events and summarize who, if anyone, was responsible for what transpired. Here is the response:

> The Black Hebrew Israelites bear the primary responsibility for instigating the conflict, while the Covington Catholic students' response, though not escalating the situation, did not defuse it either. Nathan Phillips' involvement appears to have been based on a misunderstanding, as he interpreted the students' actions as disrespectful.[2]

Take a moment to search the early stories that covered the events at the Lincoln Memorial, and you will find a glaring omission—that of the five members of the Black Hebrew Israelites. Their presence is simply not mentioned. It took days for the media to acknowledge that they were even present. Many outlets, if they did finally admit their presence, downplayed how antagonistically they were behaving. It didn't fit the narrative at the time.

*The truth, the WHOLE truth...*our courtroom oath doesn't sound so redundant when confronted with how damaging partial truth, especially when smashed together with false narrative, can be.

I'm not a mind reader, so I can't tell you exactly why the members of the Black Hebrew Israelites were left out of the coverage. And I can't say for certain why Nick was granted the ominous spotlight. What I can undoubtedly say is that 2019 was a year when ideological and political lines were being drawn. Donald Trump's first term was nearing its end, and the 2020 presidential campaign season was already at a fever pitch.

Most major news outlets, acting more like Jerry Springer than Walter Cronkite, were looking for headline-grabbing moments. A face-to-face encounter between a "privileged" white kid wearing a red MAGA hat and an older Native

American with a ceremonial drum likely felt as if it had been dropped from pundit-heaven.

So, instead of spending some time to interview witnesses or find videos in which the full context of that afternoon was presented, major news outlets—the self-described Bastion of Ethics in the United States, the Watchers of the Watchers, the Ones Who Speak Truth to Power—snatched a one-minute-long video and put Nick, red hat and all, in their crosshairs. Those crosshairs can be brutal for most. When it came to Nick, they were downright voracious. Stories began popping up describing Nick and his classmates as aggressors, calling them a hostile crowd while Phillips drummed peacefully.

In a shocking display of one-sided "journalism," many outlets reached out to Phillips for comment. He made claims that he heard chants of "build the wall" (something that absolutely cannot be heard on any of the subsequent video recordings of the incident) and went so far as to say that he was trying to protect others from the Covington students.

Pundits, celebrities, and third-rate news sites on Twitter reacted swiftly. A CNN analyst and professor at a California university tweeted about Nick, "Have you ever seen a more punchable face than this kid's?" A film producer, when speaking about the events, said, "MAGA kids go screaming, hats first, into the woodchipper." Yet another reporter tweeted that he wanted Nick, his classmates, and their parents to die.

The Secretary of the State of Kentucky at the time said that the "horrific" scene, along with the students' actions, did not reflect Kentucky's values. She went on to say, "I turn to the adults that are teaching them and those that are silently letting others promote this behavior. This is not the Kentucky I know and love. We can do better, and it starts with better leadership."

It seems everyone was rallying around the false narrative that had been quickly and haphazardly packaged up and thrown into the political winds. The communications director for Covington Catholic wrote a statement that expressed regret for the "altercation." Further piling on, the Diocese of Covington sent an apology to Mr. Phillips, condemning the students' behavior and promising that once they had fully investigated the situation, they would take additional appropriate measures (including expulsion from their private school if necessary).

As Nick was being framed as the face of evil in America, the media went on to prop up Mr. Phillips as the hero. He and others of the Indigenous People's March were given opportunity after opportunity to expound on their perspectives, describe their version of events, and editorialize to their heart's content. In multiple interviews, Mr. Phillips talked about how the MAGA attire worn by Nick and his classmates made him and others feel threatened. He made wrong claims about what they said (like the aforementioned "build the wall"). Ruth Buffalo, a Representative for the North Dakota Tribe, used the opportunity to draw comparisons across the nation at large: "The behavior shown in that video is just a snapshot of what Indigenous people have faced and are continuing to face."[3]

Picking up on the things Mr. Phillips was saying, *The New York Times* said the events had become "the latest touch point for racial and political tensions in America, with diverging views about what really had happened." The racial and political angles were too much for most outlets to ignore.

Not to be outdone by the *NYT*, *The Washington Post* wasted no time in manufacturing comparisons between the altercation and other situations involving Native American topics and political figures like Donald Trump and Elizabeth Warren. Again, leaning on only short video snippets, they speculated that Mr. Phillips was an example of how Native Americans would not be silenced. Vox breathlessly described the situation as "the nation's biggest story."

Sadly, this pseudo-news reporting began to work. The short videos were viewed millions of times within less than twenty-four hours. Celebrities, ever chasing the spotlight and trying to hitch their wagons to the hot topic of the moment (regardless of what the truth truly held), jumped in with both feet. In a state of melodrama, Alyssa Milano tweeted, "This is

Trump's America. And it brought me to tears. What are we teaching our young people? Why is this ok? How is this ok? Please help me understand. Because right now I feel like my heart is living outside of my body."

More insidiously, Kathy Griffin completely stepped outside of reality in attempting to frame all of Covington Catholic in a negative light by accusing a basketball player of "throwing up a nazi sign."[4] Not mincing words, Jim Carrey simply tweeted an image, calling Nick and his classmates "baby snakes."

News coverage was so overwhelming that even representatives for the March for Life released a statement where they characterized the students' behavior as "reprehensible."

The searing political spotlight of the United States had been firmly locked onto this story. The characters had been defined, and Nick had been chosen as the arch-villain. There was nowhere for him to hide. All because the facts were not being represented. There was little truth. The WHOLE truth lay in scattered pieces across a ludicrous narrative. And nothing but the truth had become *anything but the truth*.

Overreaction Followed by (Some) Retraction

It's fair to say that January 18th and 19th were a press feeding frenzy. Story after story, pundit after pundit, tweet after tweet—it just kept coming. Each hot take felt more egregious. More unfair and false.

If there is a silver lining to this story, it came on Sunday, January 20th. A longer video was released to the public, containing more context and free from the splicing of "choice" moments. As soon as it was released, the truth began to show through.

This video showed the Black Hebrew Israelites as they taunted everyone in the vicinity—specifically, how they had been focused on berating the Covington Catholic students. It showed how Mr. Phillips had not moved toward Nick in order to protect himself or others. Rather, it showed a more aggressive posture. It showed how Nick was not blocking anything about the Indigenous People's March. It captured no racial insults from the Covington Catholic students. No chant of "build the wall." No disrespect. Nothing racial. Nothing violent.

In fact, it showed restraint on the part of a high school-aged young man in the face of an overwhelmingly aggressive scene. There was no way around it. The media, in their desire to craft a story with a MAGA-hat-wearing villain, had gotten it very wrong. They had given a platform to the wrong person, and that platform had led to lies, insults, threats, and condemnation.

Justifications from the media began flying at near supersonic speeds. The loudest of the accusers went silent. And the retractions were done quietly, in tiny text, hidden multiple pages from the front. Tweets were taken down. A few apologies were issued.

- Kathy Griffin deleted her accusatory tweet about a Covington basketball player, but never apologized.

- *The New York Times* adjusted the title from *Boys in 'Make America Great Again' Hats Mob Native Elder at Indigenous People's March* to *Fuller Picture Emerges of Viral Video of Native American Man and Catholic Students*.[5]

- CNN changed the title of their original story from *Teens in Make America Great Again Hats Taunted a Native American Elder at the Lincoln Memorial* to *Teen in confrontation with Native American elder says he was trying to defuse the situation*.[6]

- The film producer who tweeted about throwing Nick and his classmates into a woodchipper issued an apology for his "fast, profoundly stupid tweet."[7]

- The CNN analyst and professor at a California university who called Nick "punchable" in quiet cowardice took a year to delete his tweet.[8]

- Follow-up news programs on CNN tried to deflect the blame to Twitter for allowing the original video to go viral, accusing several anonymous accounts of retweeting it in the first place. Indeed, these accusations led to the House Intelligence Committee asking Twitter to justify why the video went viral.[9]

- As the media blitzkrieg against Nick began to slow, the organizers of the March for Life rescinded their original statement condemning Nick and his Covington Catholic classmates, stating, "It is clear from new footage and additional accounts that there is more to this story than the original video captured."[10]

- Representative Thomas Massie finally broke his silence after more footage was available, saying, "In the context of everything that was going on (which the media hasn't shown), the parents and mentors of these boys should be proud, not ashamed of their kids' behavior."[11]

- After even more days had passed, Savannah Guthrie finally interviewed Nick on the *Today Show*, where Nick shared that he wished he had just walked away when Mr. Phillips approached him. He went on to say that he held no ill will toward Mr. Phillips and that he hoped they could talk at some point. (Even with all the new information, many people criticized Guthrie for giving Nick an opportunity to share his side—these same people continued to prop up Mr. Phillips even though his versions of the events became more and more unreliable).[12]

It's important to note that as the events of January 18th became more apparent, many were upset at the media's gross negligence in vetting their sources (or controlling their overreactions). Some media personalities would not give up their quick conviction of Nick. Kristin Powers of CNN doubled down, saying, "Watching all the videos (which I did) does not change the fundamental problem: the boys disrespecting an Indigenous elder." It seems she was a little too stubborn on this take. Shortly after posting, she claims to have been harassed and criticized so stringently that she closed her Twitter account. It seems that she buckled under the slightest modicum of pressure that Nick had been experiencing.

I wish this next paragraph could go on to say that Nick was able to ride off into the sunset, having been justified once the facts were finally made clear. That, sadly, is not the case. This type of defamation never goes away because there is no way to change the millions of minds who sold the initial false story. And this type of defamation lives forever on the Internet—perpetually.

I pray none of my readers experience the level of perpetual reputational harm that Nick has suffered. *Perpetual reputational harm*—don't read that as an ambiguous legal term, because it is not. A person suffering from this level of defamation will never be able to introduce himself to someone without his name ringing a bell. Every resumé or social media account, every time his name is printed on a license or an accreditation, will be tied to a universe of lies. And due to the proficiency of the media's false coverage of Nick, there will always be people who will hear his name and think *smug, snake, punchable, racist, dangerous.* There will be people who would relish the opportunity, even to this day, to undermine Nick as he tries to build a life for himself and his family. I have seen these hateful reactions a dozen times from people I believed otherwise to be reasonable. It is mystifying.

Yes, the truth came out. But none of it outweighed the damage the media caused.

Here is why this matters—Nick's is not a unique situation. This happens more often than we know. The media knows that they can fly fast and loose regarding details. They know they are able to say anything they want, and the second they're called on it, they can quietly change a few things in a title or delete a post from a few accounts. They can throw up their hands and say, I *was just my opinion; I wasn't presenting facts.* They can say, *I'm an entertainer, not any sort of authority figure—It's not my fault people choose to put so much stock in what I say.* If things get too hot for them, they can stand with indignance and declare the importance of a free press or wave around the First Amendment and accuse the victims of their slander of trying to silence or, worse, censor them.

They can do this because they have been empowered time and time again by a judicial system that refuses to hold them accountable. I have often said that Nick deserved his day in court. While that is true, as I look around at how people are being canceled and defamed so easily, I think it goes beyond Nick. Yes, he deserved his day in court. But more importantly, WE needed him to have his day in court. However, the system of laws and judicial precedent Nick faced would not allow that to happen. Appeal after appeal, all the way up to the Supreme Court, the judicial system aligned itself with the interests of the media corporations and kept this case from appearing in front of a jury. The laws on defamation once protected the weak, but now they protect the powerful elites that run our country. Each decision in Nick's case defended multibillion-dollar companies protected by decades of law favoring the media. Nick's case is a missed opportunity to not only right the wrong that had happened to Nick, but to push back on the media's decades of precedential power. Today, the law of defamation promotes and protects a culture where truth is less important than the narrative—where facts matter less than the emotional reaction of the most famous person in the conversation.

If you're asking, *What can we do to stop this from happening?* Or if you're feeling just a little bit more uneasy about the state of our justice system when it comes to defamation, then I've accomplished my goal with this chapter We need to know the score. We also need to understand that the rules by which this game is being played are not the rules we think they are. When we have a judicial system guarded by decades of precedent, we can't rest on the idea that all wrongs will be righted once the truth, the whole truth, and nothing but the truth is revealed.

All, however, is not lost. A wise man once said that when we understand how the positions operate, then we can master the game. This is a winnable game. Truth and fact do indeed matter, and they are just as powerful as ever. Equally important is understanding how the game is being played against us, both from the media and politicians. Often, these two players work in tandem, blocking and tackling in ways that create enough confusion that they can reach the goal unabated. It's not a complex playbook. They really only have a few plays.

Let's take a look at the media.

Chapter Notes

1 "Native American Elder Mocked by Young Donald Trump Supporters in Maga Hats? It's Not That Simple," ABC News, last modified Sun 20 Jan 2019, 2019, accessed May 24, 2024, https://www.abc.net.au/news/2019-01-21/native-american-surrounded-maga-trump-supporters-what-happened/10730988.

2 ChatGPT, Response to Sandmann Review (OpenAI, 2024).

3 Adam Beam, and Brian Melley, "Students in 'Maga' Hats Mock Native American after Rally," last modified Jan 20, 2019, 2019, accessed May 24, 2024, https://www.pbs.org/newshour/nation/students-in-maga-hats-mock-native-american-after-rally.

4 This tweet has since been deleted, and no reference can be provided. However, it can be found on several media outlets.

5 Sarah Mervosh and Emily S. Rueb, "Fuller Picture Emerges of Viral Video of Native American Man and Catholic Students," The New York Times, 2019, accessed May 2024, 2024, https://www.nytimes.com/2019/01/20/us/nathan-phillips-covington.html.

6 David Williams, and Emanuella Grinberg, "Teen in Confrontation with Native American Elder Says He Was Trying to Defuse the Situation," last modified Jan 23, 2019, 2019, accessed MAY 24, 2024, https://www.cnn.com/2019/01/19/us/teens-mock-native-elder-trnd/index.html.

7 Itay Hod, and Jon Levine, "Https://Www.Thewrap.Com/Film-Producer-Jack-Morrissey-Apologizes-for-Deleted-Covington-Woodchipper-Tweet/," last modified Jan 21, 2019, 2019, accessed May 24, 2024, https://www.thewrap.com/film-producer-jack-morrissey-apologizes-for-deleted-covington-woodchipper-tweet/.

8 Valerie Richardson, "Reza Aslan 'Likely' to Be Sued over Now-Deleted 'Punchable Face' Tweet: Sandmann Attorney," last modified Jan 13, 2020, 2020, accessed May 24, 2024, https://www.washingtontimes.com/news/2020/jan/13/reza-aslan-likely-be-sued-over-now-deleted-punchab/.

9 Katie Reilly, "The Viral Lincoln Memorial Confrontation Shows We're Ill-Equipped to Deal with Online Disinformation," last modified Jan 23, 2019, 2019, accessed May 24, 2024, https://time.com/5509832/covington-catholic-nathan-phillips-social-media-division/.

10 March for Life (@March_for_Life), X (Twitter), 6:48 PM · Jan 20, 2019, 2019, https://x.com/March_for_Life/status/1087179995414519810.

11 "Rep. Massie Defends Cov Cath Students: 'It Is My Honor to Represent Them'," last modified Jan 20, 2019, 2019, accessed May 24, 2024, https://www.wlwt.com/article/rep-massie-defends-cov-cath-students-its-my-honor-to-represent-them/25970945.

12 Eun Kyung Kim, "Nick Sandmann on Encounter with Nathan Phillips: 'I Wish I Would've Walked Away'," last modified Jan 23, 2019, 2019, accessed May 24, 2024, https://www.today.com/news/nick-sandmann-interview-today-show-s-savannah-guthrie-encounter-native-t147242.

YOUR SILENCE IS THEIR GOAL

THE ANATOMY OF A MEDIA HIT JOB

"The dumbing down of America is most evident in the slow decay of substantive content in the enormously influential media..."
- Carl Sagan

A ccording to Pew Research, fifty percent of Americans consider "made-up news" a more significant issue than many other key issues impacting them.[1] Given how irresponsible the media has become when reporting hearsay and inflammatory stories without fact-checking or deeper investigation, I'm surprised that number isn't higher. With the ever-increasing demand for content and the competitive landscape for attention, news outlets are under pressure to create stories that demand attention.

Humanity has never had more access to information than we do now. Virtually anything we want is at our fingertips within seconds of needing it. But with that access comes the need for considerable discernment. While it would be great if everyone in the media took responsibility to report information with an even and honest hand, that is sadly not the case. I also don't believe that having fact-checkers or stringent control over what can be said is the answer (in fact, I will be discussing how damaging fact-checkers have been in the defamatory landscape in a future chapter).

I believe the responsibility lies with us, the consumers. We have been given the ability to reason and research. We navigate our daily lives in a way that requires us to take in information and make important decisions. And when something says one thing but demonstrates another, we stop and evaluate.

For example, imagine you're hiking in the Arizona desert when you come upon a snake stretched across the trail in front of you. The snake is long enough that its head is obscured under a nearby bush, and its tail hasn't yet emerged from behind a rock on the other side of the trail. It has the markings of the legendary Rattlesnake, but you know other harmless snakes share the same markings—quite the quandary.

Do you keep walking and hope it's not venomous? Or turn around and run for fear of the neurotoxin it may deliver to you if you try to step over it? It's more likely you'd choose a third option. You'd wait, at a safe distance, for the snake to move so you could see the shape of its head, or whether it has rattles on its tail. To state it differently, you would wait for the full context of the situation.

This is the same tactic we should take when being presented with information by the media. One side of the media may want to obscure the head and tail of the snake so that you don't see how dangerously one of their darlings in government is behaving. The other side may try to scare you by standing in the corner, shaking a rattle, and attributing it to someone not aligned with their ideology. They're not the keepers of the information. Most of the time, if we're willing, we will come to a better understanding of a situation than they could present. We just have to take the time to observe the snake.

The principles of thorough fact-checking, balanced reporting, and the discernment of truth are especially vital when news involves the average citizen. For many individuals, an encounter with the media might be a singular event, yet it can have lasting effects on their reputation and daily life. Inaccurate or biased reporting can misinform public opinion, exacerbate social divisions, and erode trust in media sources. When the media rush to publish without sufficient verification, they risk spreading misinformation that can be damaging and difficult to correct.

As consumers, our role is not passive. We must engage critically with the information presented to us, questioning and researching rather than accepting it at face value. This active engagement helps uphold the integrity of our information ecosystem, ensuring that as we navigate vast amounts of data, we prioritize truth and context over sensationalism and haste. Thus, by fostering a culture of critical consumption and demanding higher standards from media outlets, we protect not only ourselves but the fabric of our society from the distortions of "made-up news."

It Can Happen to Anyone

A friend of mine (let's refer to him as "Jim") was troubled recently. About halfway through her semester, his daughter (we will call her "Mary"), a fifth-grader, came home from school grumpier than usual. At first, the typical suspects for a fifth-grader were discussed—"Are you having a hard time with a particular subject? Are you and your friends getting along?" And the dreaded, "Is there a boy being mean to you?" But everything was fine, so Jim dug deeper.

It became apparent that Mary was frustrated with her teacher. This was highly uncharacteristic for his straight-A daughter, who had a great relationship with every teacher she had. The news about Mary's frustration was shocking, to say the least. There had been no notes home from her teacher, and Jim's wife, a weekly volunteer in the classroom, had seen nothing out of the ordinary.

Finally, after almost every other possibility had been exhausted, Mary said, "He keeps talking about personal stuff." She described how her teacher was very excited to share that he was dating another man and that he had never been more in love. Mary felt uncomfortable because she felt like the relationship was becoming increasingly central to classroom discussions.

At first, Jim and his wife told Mary that it was ok. They assumed her teacher's initial excitement for a new relationship would fade, and the classroom would settle back into the learning environment it had been previously. Privately, they were frustrated that Mary's teacher was not more temperate with topics that fell outside the district's curriculum—something he had been doing earlier in the year regarding other topics, like religion.

Unfortunately, Mary's teacher not only continued his focus on his relationship—he made it more and more a focus of the class. He would share, starry-eyed, details of their dates. Then, in tears, he would share about how mean some of his friends were being because they disapproved of the homosexual relationship. It got so bad that the teacher began showing up late with stories of how tired or stressed he was because of unaccepting people. A Pride flag appeared one day, followed by more rainbows and stories.

Many of you reading this can probably relate to Jim's experience. The education landscape in America has been turned into a battlefield for LGBTQIA+ rights. Several states have enacted laws that require the subject and its history to be taught in the classroom, with teachers being encouraged to share their struggles and personal experiences. In contrast, a record number of topic-limiting bills were introduced in 2023, with at least 510 such bills across various states.[2]

These bills often focus on education and healthcare, with many aiming to regulate discussions around gender identity and sexuality in schools. For instance, the so-called "Don't Say Gay" laws, like those expanded in Florida, restrict classroom discussions on sexual orientation and gender identity.[3] The argument is that it exposes young minds to decisions and concepts that should be discussed later in adulthood. It is really not about the nature of the relationship, but about keeping the classroom focused on education.

Millions of parents around the country have faced Jim's situation and have had to decide for themselves how to respond. In this polarized modern world, most concerned parents either choose to put up with the situation, gritting their teeth and bearing it, or employ a bombastic tirade to a school board or social media outlet. Neither option was acceptable for Jim and his wife. They attempted to resolve the matter as quietly and professionally as possible.

After praying for guidance, Jim spoke privately with the school's principal and learned that other parents were raising similar concerns. The principal assured him the administration was taking steps to curb the behavior, but nothing changed. Mary's teacher continued to bring up his relationship—even encouraging the children in his class to stand up for "people like him" and to "courageously come out" if they thought they should.

Despite the constant presence of her teacher's relationship, they found a way to continue through the rest of the year. Mary ended fifth grade with her usual straight As, but her daily consternation was as high as ever. So, Jim wrote Mary's teacher a letter at the end of the year. There was no anger in the letter. There was no mention of Jim's personal stance toward homosexual relationships. The central thesis was simple: "Your effectiveness as a teacher is best served by not making your personal life the central focus of the class."

Jim sent the letter on the last day of school after the final bell had rung. He received no response, and he pursued the matter no further. They had made it through and professionally stood their ground.

A year went by, and the issue faded into memory.

And then, out of nowhere, a reporter from a local intersectionally-focused publication reached out to Jim. The teacher was claiming that the school had forced him out (offering him a large severance for his silence) and that it was due to pressure from "closed-minded, conservative Christian parents." Jim was presented as the ringleader and told he would be named in an upcoming article. He was even told his personal letter to the teacher could be quoted or printed in full, and that it clearly demonstrated that Jim's problem was that the teacher was a homosexual.

The hit job was in full swing, and Jim had been blindsided. Without notice and unable to clarify his stance, he was squarely in the crosshairs of a media hit job. Something that has become all too common. It seems that the more ideologically motivated our society becomes, what would have been considered normal is being used against unsuspecting people in schools, workplaces, public forums, and in the media. The nature of these hit jobs is consistent. The playbook used, while powerful, is predictable. In many cases, if someone is committed to defaming you, the experience will be stressful, damaging, confusing, costly, and require you to fight as hard as you can to try to mitigate the full impact of it.

Fortunately for Jim, he had some experience in these matters and immediately sought legal counsel. Following precise defamation law principles, a strongly worded statement was drafted and sent to the media outlet. To date, they have not run the story. I wish that this was how the story ended for most folks, but sadly, it is not the case.

I hope you never find yourself in the midst of a defamatory attack, but as the world spins farther and farther out of control, the faster you can spot how defamation begins and gains momentum, the better off you'll be. In addition to the rest of this chapter, I have included a guide in the appendix to help those who find themselves in defamation crosshairs. It is NOT a substitute for legal counsel, but it is a great place to start.

The more significant lesson is that the laws offer you little protection. If a media entity runs a story about a "bigoted" parent, that parent faces a tough uphill battle to protect his family's reputation. This means that reporters can and often do act with impunity. They know they can get away with calling someone a bigot or a racist, and then stand smugly behind their lawyer's letter saying that this was a matter of public concern, it's just this reporter's opinion, or it's truthful and not defamatory. All the while, the parent is being attacked on social media, has a news truck parked in front of his house, and has his friends and neighbors avoiding contact.

What if this parent is a community leader? Well, the next thing to happen is that the boards and commissions he serves on disinvite him from service. Then, the banks don't answer his calls, and finally, his business drops off. What if a college scholarship athlete is caught up in a defamatory attack? She might have her coach tell her she will be removed from the team, which means losing her scholarship. This happens all of the time. That is why it is so important to be able to spot an attack coming.

Cancel Culture Hit Jobs

There is a viral video floating around where two groups of people, one dressed in black and the other in white, run around a room, passing basketballs back and forth.[4] The goal for the viewer on the first view is to count how many times the team in black passes their basketball to each other. On the second run-through, the viewer must count the number of passes for the team in white. It sounds simple enough to accomplish, but not so easy to execute. The teams are tightly packed together, the players constantly move in random directions, and there's not much time to prepare mentally before the task begins.

What really gets you, however, is when the video pauses after a second loop and asks, "Now, how many of you saw the dancing gorilla?" The video plays a third time, and sure enough, about five seconds into the session, a person dressed as a gorilla enters the melee and dances his way through the rest of the video. If you go back to the first and second run-throughs, you see the exact same dancing gorilla. In your desire to follow directions, you missed a shockingly obvious element of the video.

It's a masterful example of how we can miss something right in front of us if we are focusing on the wrong thing. It's also a stellar illustration of how powerful misdirection can be on an unsuspecting audience. If the directions had been to spot all the weird things happening in the group, well, the gorilla would be front and center. But when the creators tell you to watch a basketball, a gorilla is the last thing on your mind.

This is the exact same tactic employed in defamation. Whether it's the media, an administration, or whoever is executing the hit job, the goal will be misdirection from the start. If they can be the first to craft a damning narrative, the rest falls neatly into place. But we need to learn not to follow their directions and instead become experts at spotting the dancing gorilla. That is, we need to learn how to see both the hallmarks and anatomy of the hit job.

The Hallmarks of a Hit Job

Let's demystify some of the tried-and-true tactics the media uses when presenting narratives that are intended to persuade us one way or the other. We can frequently identify hit jobs by evaluating them in three categories.

An Oversimplified Presentation

The twenty-four-hour news cycle is repetitive by nature. It has to be. Most of the time, there really isn't enough going on across the country to justify hyped-up news anchors breathlessly reporting on a situation with slick graphics sliding across the screen in the background. To keep their viewers glued to the screen, they repeat the same topics, with slightly different takes from different anchors. The tactics of a hit job follow a similar pattern.

Given how easily situations can be captured with video from a cell phone, most hit jobs will have some video associated with them. However, if you're only being offered a short snippet of a situation, a larger context is almost certainly being obscured. If the video snippet being presented starts when the altercation has already begun (if people are already yelling or a physical confrontation is one of the first things you see), we need to ask what events led to the confrontation.

If the video abruptly cuts off before any type of resolution, why weren't the next thirty seconds also shown? And, because it's become so common for people to pull out their phones to record situations (if there's only one single video being used), we need to understand why there aren't other corroborating videos being brought forward as proof. I realize there are exceptions to all of these scenarios. Sometimes, a situation isn't captured until it's already escalated, for example. Or maybe there's only one video available at the moment. I get it; we won't always have a multi-angled, perfectly steady video of every situation.

But suppose there truly is only one video available. In that case, it's quite possible the media has picked up the story very early and may be running with it before fully vetting the facts (this is precisely what happened to Nick Sandmann). Either the media is being irresponsible, or they are beginning to craft a narrative that will be used to cancel someone. Either way, we must be aware and hold back until we know more.

Another element to consider is to whom the media gives voice. As the story progresses, they will inevitably want to interview someone impacted by the event in question. Watch to see who gets the most airtime. Are they only interviewing representatives of the protesters who were arrested? Do we only hear from the tearful mother of the teenager who was tragically shot during a traffic stop? If the media acts with pure intent, they will seek to provide perspectives from all sides involved. If the "other" side is nowhere to be found (or only given a clipped video statement), an agenda may be at play.

Along with truncated context and one-sided interviews, the presentation of the hit job will be rounded out with people claiming to have internal knowledge of the situation, or "experts" who are brought in to analyze the story. Pay close attention to how these folks speak. They will rarely add factual information to the story. Instead, they will introduce more opinion than fact, which almost always serves to add tangles to the narrative instead of providing a better understanding. All of these tactics in presenting the situation hook an audience through more emotion than fact and establish the narrative they want to be presented.

Emotional Puppet Mastering

As the hit job progresses in the media, the pundits and talking heads will lead the way in driving the false narrative, mainly by injecting as much emotion into the coverage as they can. Be mindful of the language incorporated into their monologues, and how they refer to the various individuals involved in the story.

Like it or not, certain words and phrases immediately impact how we react to them, and the effect isn't always outward. Often, the use of slanderous words serves to wear folks down. If someone is labeled over and over again as a bigot, most will eventually come to see that person in a negative light. Just like we discussed above, buzzwords and insulting language are used in media hit jobs as a powerful tool to frame the story in the terms they want you to believe. Look for these phrases when a host introduces or wraps the segment, or when panel members are having a lively discussion. Social media will be flush with them as more ideological allies join the storm.

A close cousin to insults and harsh labels is the tactic of equating the "villain" of a hit job with another person or group that is already widely accepted as verboten. If the person in question is being called a Nazi or being compared to Stalin, for example, there is likely much more to the story. Most of the time, these types of comparisons will be used quickly as shorthand to evoke a spike of emotion in the viewer. Remember, this is a war of attrition, and if the media can label their villain in one breath with an insulting buzzword and, in the next breath, equate them to Pol Pot, they will happily do so.

If we are not careful, eventually, those earworms will wiggle their way deep enough into our subconscious that we will find ourselves reacting emotionally rather than with a more rational approach.

Looking Strong, Acting Weak

Allegedly. Apparently. Supposed. Listen to any hit job, and you will hear these terms often. Most people will listen to similar terms and immediately assume that the personality using them is being careful, possibly even respectful, by leaving room for future information that may change the narrative. In legal terms, that may be true—we've already discussed the importance of fact vs. opinion—but another element is at play. Just like John Stewart throwing his hands in the air and claiming that nobody should take him seriously because his show is on a comedy channel, pundits and advocate journalists can use these types of terms as a shield behind which to hide.

While claiming they're even-handed, they can simultaneously label their "villain" with any term they see fit. We hear it all the time: *This alleged domestic terrorist. In what looks to be an apparent attempt to undermine democracy.* As soon as a small disclaimer is added to a phrase, the person coordinating the hit job can abdicate all responsibility. *I didn't call them a domestic terrorist,* they will say; *I was just offering an opinion of what might be happening.* The most insidious aspect of this tactic is that incorporating such terms used to be an actual safe haven for innocent people. There was a time when "allegedly" was a clear indicator that the person being discussed was still innocent. Sadly, members of the media and most politicians have turned that dynamic on its head. Most people don't even register these terms anymore. They just get caught up in the narrative.

The Anatomy of a Hit Job

As important as it is to recognize when you're about to be in the crosshairs of an attack, it's equally important to be able to recognize when the media is trying to fool us with one of their contrived and orchestrated attacks on someone else. Remember, if we're not being attacked by a hit job, we're the ones that the media, and those wielding the cancel culture banner, are trying to influence. You can usually spot the anatomy of a hit job by watching for these three stages.

Springing the Trap—Naming & Framing a Situation

Everything starts with some sort of encounter. A disagreement, a confrontation—something that highlights a dispute or misalignment between you and someone else. And since most of us live in a relatively calm environment, it will simultaneously seem out of the ordinary, but often brief.

Slightly uncomfortable, but likely not earth-shattering. You need to understand that most people who find themselves in these situations aren't looking for a fight. They're not trying to make some giant statement. They are usually just navigating their way through the world in a way that, for all intents and purposes, aligns with what a normal society would expect.

Most often, the initial disagreement will be regarding some agenda being pushed (either by the individual or a larger organization). Look no further than the ever-growing DEI policies in corporate environments, the demand not to just accept but advocate for LGBTQIA+ ideals in public schools, or a myriad of other topics that demand zero deviation from a single way of thinking. In short, if you are deemed to have broken THEIR rules (not THE rules), you will become a target.

I don't point this out in an attempt to dissuade anybody from engaging in these topics or to induce fear. On the contrary, it's essential that whatever you believe about these topics, you should be able to express yourself freely (even if I disagree with you). The silencing of dissenting voices is one of the goals of defamation. I'm merely pointing out the areas where you're more likely to find yourself embattled.

The first thing that will happen is the "offended" party will try to name and frame the issue from their perspective. They will almost certainly begin using buzzwords (racist, bigot, misogynist) to try to label your actions while simultaneously focusing on one (probably minor) part of the situation. Did you disagree a little too fast? You'll be framed as closed-minded, defensive, and aggressive.

Did you show any level of frustration? Well, you'll be labeled as angry, violent, and out of control. A key point to understand is that your *reaction* to this attempt to frame you will be scrutinized as much, if not more, than whatever the initial confrontation was.

Every good villain (that's you) needs a relatable victim (that could be the person naming and framing you or some "group" of people who could be hurt or impacted by the behavior for which you're being framed). Identifying a victim is key in this phase because it allows for two important tactics.

Tactic One: Engage the Emotions. If there is a victim to whom others can relate, it allows for blatant and manipulative statements that are devoid of fact and flush with comparisons to other situations, or hyperbolic "what if" statements (*If this person could cause such harm to our victim, what other heinous things might they be capable of?*). Keep in mind that victimhood can be played in a couple of different ways.

There is the victim who is "weak" and being oppressed by the "aggressive" and "domineering" abuser. Then there's the "righteous" victim who "boldly" and "defiantly" stands against someone in power who is "misusing" their status to cheat and swindle more power from those who truly deserve it. But make no mistake—regardless of the type of victim behavior, all of it is designed to falsely frame you or your actions in the worst possible light.

Tactic Two: Control the Narrative. Once a victim has been established and the focus has turned to emotions, the facts will get turned on their heads. At this point, the initial encounter will never again be presented from the largest possible context. In other words, the WHOLE TRUTH will be thrown from the window as this runaway defamation train leaves the station. The whole situation will be chopped up into small, context-free snippets that can be hand-picked depending on the questions or audience.

However, there will be one detail that will be emphasized time and time again. This detail will be repeated and no matter what else you do, the narrative will continuously revolve around this one detail. It is the rallying cry, and it will be the thing that allows the whole situation to be used to gain momentum.

There it is. The trap has been sprung—the stage is primed for the next step.

Tightening the Snares—Seeking Allies

At this point in the hit job, the tension will be high enough to expand as far as possible. This could be instantaneous—a person may start a livestream, try to engage social media, or the "victim" may begin raising their voice in an office setting to draw attention as the wounded party. If not instantaneously, they may seek allies through gossip, emailing a manager, or contacting the media. Fitting perfectly with trying to control the narrative, no matter how they begin to draw in supporters, their story will have insufficient context, be full of emotional accusation, and lack any attempt to be moderate.

Perhaps the saddest part of this process is that they will find allies quickly and easily. Most people in our culture have been conditioned to accept and align with this type of behavior. Peers will either distance themselves to "not cause waves," or they will want to stand up for the one claiming to be oppressed.

Managers will jump in with little to no additional questions, fearing an HR nightmare. School administrators, terrified of lawsuits or bad press, will turn authoritative as quickly as possible. The media, smelling high ratings and the furthering of an ideological platform, will seek to enhance the drama.

And because the narrative will have already been laid out, the allies will fall neatly in step with it. Questions from managers/administration will be stated with accusatory tones or will assume a wrong motive. Reporters will start digging for anything else that might be used to lay blame or cause you shame.

If the hit job gets big enough, even third parties will jump into the fray with tangential salvos designed to undermine you (See Kathy Griffin's heinous tweet about Covington Catholic's basketball team that I mentioned earlier in the book as an example).

As more allies are identified and more people buy the narrative, the slanderous terms will continue to fly. The questions will stop. Accusatory tones will be replaced with straightforward accusations. Context will have been completely erased.

The penultimate moment of this phase will come when those in authority have been completely won over. There will no longer be even the slightest appearance of a desire to "get to the bottom" of the situation. At this point, a voracious advocate for the "victim" will emerge. Regardless of how minimized your point of view initially was, your voice will be completely stripped from you. Any attempt to justify yourself or point back to the true context will be taken as you trying to justify what will have been labeled as "wrong behavior."

At this point, the hit job has been executed. Your reputation will be in tatters—potentially irrevocably. The only question left is how far they will push the hit job. How will the attack on you be used to establish more power?

Going in for the Kill—Punishment & Retribution

It is important to remember that a defamatory hit job like this is rarely a personal attack. I realize the irony of that statement because defamation has incredibly personal ramifications. Regardless, these hit jobs are almost always in service of furthering a worldview or establishing control over a group of people. Sometimes, it is no more than trying to settle the score, where one person sees an opportunity to get back at another person at work, school, or on the athletic field.

When such aggressive ideologies are at play, you're no longer seen as a person. You are an object on a gameboard, meant to be maneuvered in whatever manner the Game Master desires. So the question becomes, what outcome is the most desired from the hit job?

Power and authority. Cancel culture thrives on establishing power and authority. Don't say the right thing? Lose your job. Vote the wrong way? You're not fit for your position anymore. Follow that social account? Your spot on the board is in jeopardy. And what's the outcome of operating this way? Forced compliance. Silence. Fear.

When a hit job has fully developed, it will be time to administer punishment and seek retribution. In the case of Nick Sandmann, the punishment came at the hands of millions of social media users and prominent media outlets. The retribution was in calling for his harm (whether through formal channels like expulsion or by way of the mob through threats of violence). But he was just the billboard. He was just the commercial for millions of other parents. The message? *If it happened to Nick, it can happen to your family. Take that hat off and fall in line with what we want, or your child will be next.* The perpetrators of these hit jobs will deliver their message of compliance in a couple of unmistakable ways.

The first avenue will be to have you cower publicly. Forget what really happened—that's not important. What's important is whether you will bend the knee by apologizing for whatever behavior you've been accused of or denouncing the ideology that led to the initial confrontation. They want you to be subservient because that's the message.

If you remain subservient to us, you will avoid pain. They will seek this alignment so aggressively that you may even find yourself on a stage in front of your co-workers or a camera, being asked to read a pre-written statement. Remember, you're not nearly as important in the cancel culture environment as how others view your treatment and your eventual response.

An even more desirable outcome for the folks engineering these types of hit jobs is for you not only to denounce what happened, but also fully align yourself with the very people attacking you. If they can inflict enough pain so that you're willing to restructure your belief system, then their message is even stronger. *Those who obey our rules won't have to go through this.*

And, if you don't relent? What happens if you push back too hard and keep hold of the truth despite the pain? Loss of status. Loss of a job. Crucifixion by way of even more media coverage. I have encountered prominent executives, professionals, scholarship athletes, and educators who have lost their jobs or scholarships for crossing a red line they did not even know existed. One wrong word can lead to complaints from the dean's or coach's offices.

Often, these cancellations terminate a person's career so that they can't get anything other than a minimum-wage position. I have seen business owners who have gone bankrupt and families who have had to move because their reputation and kids' safety have been absolutely compromised. Again, the message is clear. *If you don't relent to our way of thinking, your life will end in ruin.*

Regardless of how you respond, you will have suffered greatly, and their message of *Submit or else* will have been delivered—not just to you but to everyone in America.

We Are in a Battle

We just went through a play-by-play of how a hit job is structured from inception through execution all the way to the final outcome. These hit jobs, accomplished through the ubiquity of cancel culture, are powerful. They start fast, gain momentum even faster, and can leave you disoriented, confused, financially compromised, and reputationally damaged. But it is not a hopeless situation.

As I said at the start of this chapter, if we can spot the playbook, we don't have to be disoriented. If we know the tactics, we can play offense instead of being forced into defense. One of the strongest ways of doing this is identifying and calling out a hit job when we see it.

We're in a battle. Whether we're unlucky enough to be the subject of a hit job or we're being manipulated into accepting the narrative of one, the all-out assault for what is true is in full swing. As you reflect on the tactics mentioned above, I urge you not to simply imagine the logo of the news channel or social media account you least agree with as an example of what I am talking about. Sure, it's easier to point out what we disagree with and identify when they act in bad faith. But this is a playbook used by all sides and on every front.

Ultimately, as these elements are used by those with the loudest microphones, the gap between everyday citizens widens. That's truly what's at stake here. We can't just choose a side and cheer when our side executes a hit job well, or jeer when we see a hit job from the other side. If we do that, we're still being manipulated—it just means we're in on it because we see what's going on.

Instead, we need to watch in a way that doesn't just count the basketball passes we're told to count. We need to watch for the person dancing in the gorilla suit and point it out every time we see it.

Chapter Notes

1 Amy Mitchell et al., "Many Americans Say Made-up News Is a Critical Problem That Needs to Be Fixed," Pew Research Center, 2019, accessed May 24, 2024, https://www.pewresearch.org/journalism/2019/06/05/many-americans-say-made-up-news-is-a-critical-problem-that-needs-to-be-fixed/.

2 Annette Choi, "Record Number of Anti-Lgbtq Bills Were Introduced in 2023," last modified Jan 22, 2024, 2023, accessed May 24, 2024, https://www.cnn.com/politics/anti-lgbtq-plus-state-bill-rights-dg/index.html.

3 Jo Yurcaba, "Over 30 New Lgbtq Education Laws Are in Effect as Students Go Back to School," last modified Aug 30, 2023, 2023, accessed May 24, 2024, https://www.nbcnews.com/nbc-out/out-politics-and-policy/30-new-lgbtq-education-laws-are-effect-students-go-back-school-rcna101897.

4 Daniel Simons. "Selective Attention Test", YouTube Video, 2010, 1:21, https://www.youtube.com/watch?v=vJG698U2Mvo.

BURNING DOWN THE PLATFORM

HOW MEDIA AND BIG TECH SILENCE OPPOSITION

"Four hostile newspapers are more to
be feared than a thousand bayonets."
- Napoleon Bonaparte

I t's never been truer than now—those who control the narrative control the actions of the populace. As we saw in the previous chapter, this desire for control often leads to ordinary people like you and me being targeted, attacked, maligned, canceled, and potentially put in harm's way. But what happens when a person gains prominence who has not succumbed to the ethos of those seeking to push an agenda of control and compliance?

There used to be tight control over who had access to the national microphone. Mega corporations with power over large television channels and newspaper publications could

...und-pick a perfectly quaffed news anchor and give them a tightly edited script from which to present the news (and a carefully cultivated ideological perspective). This tactic is still employed today—look no further than the chilling Deadspin video[1] from a few years ago, which combined clips of dozens of news stations from across the country reading word-for-word from a script about the dangers of independent media. One is forced to consider how often we have been spoon-fed story after story and monologue after monologue while consuming the "news" we've been told was so important in a free society.

The difference now is that there *are* independent personalities who have gained influence due to the rise of technologies like social media, blogging/podcast platforms, and video streaming providers. Some of these personalities provide a strong antithesis to those who have so easily manipulated the narrative for so long. And, true to any empire facing a potential extinction, these large conglomerates will not surrender their influence easily.

Just like a dog returning to its vomit, these corporations often return to the defamation strategy that has been so successful for them in the past. Mind you, some of the tactics we highlighted in the last chapter are different—when attacking an established personality, they can't just invent a narrative out of the blue—but the outcome they seek is identical: *Silence the dissenter*. They first must take the platform and burn it to the ground.

The Case of Candace Owens

History will look back on the year 2020 with great interest. I don't think it's a stretch to expect colleges to offer entire majors that focus solely on the upheaval we saw as COVID-19, the presidential election, and a myriad of social issues raged across our nation. As major media outlets offered round-the-clock coverage of city-wide riots while simultaneously interviewing government officials who told us to stay inside for fear of a global pandemic, a small, vocal, and increasingly significant group of people emerged who offered dissenting opinions regarding the best way to navigate such a strange set of circumstances. One of the loudest voices in this group was Candace Owens.

Mrs. Owens is a perfect example of someone who worked outside the traditional path to become prominent in public conversation. In 2017, she uploaded her first politically focused video to YouTube, ironically enough, speaking out against cyberbullying. Her views struck a chord with people, and she began to build a followership. At any other time, Owens would have been celebrated as a strong African American woman who bucked the odds to raise her voice above the overcrowded landscape of pundits and simpleminded personalities polluting the political scene.

However, her conservative views didn't match most of the mainstream media. Nevertheless, her influence continued to grow. Her shrewd understanding of social media, clear and concise perspective, and willingness to ask the questions nobody else would ask drew millions of people to her. She's an accomplished author, the leader and co-founder of Blexit (an organization that seeks to promote economic independence and individual freedom, strengthen the nuclear family, and foster a deeper appreciation for patriotism in Black American culture),[2] has been, until recently, a key contributor to *The Daily Wire*, and runs incredibly successful social media accounts.

As her influence grew, the attacks on Owens also began to ratchet up. She was often labeled as a conspiracy theorist, radical, and puppet of the Right-Wing. Still, none of those feeble attempts were successful in suppressing her prominence on the national stage. Her platform needed to be removed from her, and her questioning of the way COVID-19 was being reported proved the perfect opportunity.

In late March of 2020, while the world was still reeling over what to make of COVID-19, there were a lot of questions about how information was being presented. An informed populace is always a more robust and well-equipped populace, but strange things were beginning to happen throughout national media. Terms like "trust the science" and hockey-stick-type graphs showing the growth of the new and potentially deadly virus were everywhere you looked. It seemed there was a virologist around every corner.

We were being told that there needed to be one overarching voice from which we were to get our information —and that position was held by the mainstream media. As proof, there were videos across YouTube offering super-cuts of broadcast after broadcast berating their viewers, telling them, "Don't do your own research," when it came to understanding the various pieces of information being collated about COVID-19. So, when Owens dared to point to data being published by the CDC and ask why it looked strange, it caused a firestorm.

One of the most powerful platforms from which Mrs. Owens communicated with her followers was Facebook. As the pandemic gained momentum, both in how it spread and how much media attention it garnered, it was natural for her to weigh in via Facebook on what she saw. On March 29, 2020, Owens published a post via her Facebook page outlining facts from the CDC and her opinion surrounding the method U.S. government officials used to count the COVID-19 pandemic death toll (the "First Facebook Post").

Mirroring an argument made in several publications by numerous commentators and expert analysts, she argued that how the government measured the cause of death overstated the extent and danger of the COVID-19 pandemic. It read:

> Important information for everyone to know about #coronavirus. Obesity is the number 1 killer in America. Right now, they are giving everyone who dies a Covid-19 lab test. If people die from heart disease, but were asymptomatic carriers of Covid-19, their deaths are counted toward the total. Same with other viruses an[d] illnesses. I am an asthmatic. If I die from an asthma attack today, and it is determined that I have Covid-19 in my system at the time of death, my death counts as "complications from coronavirus," even if I never had any symptoms. They are trying desperately to get the numbers they need to justify this pandemic response. Below is an article that explains how they are manipulating deaths. I spent all day today trying to look up daily death rates for any other diseases. You can't get it anywhere. They are reporting ONLY on coronavirus deaths. I suspect if we begin to demand the daily death toll numbers for heart disease, we will observe a deep decline. I am most interested in NYC overall deaths for this past month (Not just from Covid-19). If anyone knows where we can get this information, please let me know. They seem to be locking it down. If they can tell us how many

people are dying from coronavirus daily— why can't they tell us how many people are dying otherwise?" ([How deadly is the coronavirus? It's still far from clear](https://www.spectator.co.uk/article/The-evidence-on-Covid-19-is-not-as-clear-as-we-think/))[3]

Given the heavy push by the media to only believe the narrative they were peddling, this post caught the attention of one of Facebook's fact-checker organizations, *Lead Stories*.

Fact-checking organizations were first instituted by Meta (Facebook's parent organization) in 2016 in an effort "to identify and address viral misinformation, particularly clear hoaxes that have no basis in fact."[4] While Facebook claims that each organization approaches its review and eventual rulings of user posts and advertisements with an unbiased perspective, it has been widely criticized for leaning heavily toward progressive agendas in both the content it focuses on and the verdicts it passes.[5]

After the First Facebook Post from Mrs. Owens, *Lead Stories* published a story titled *Fact-Check: COVID-19 NOT Being Blamed For Deaths Primarily Due To Unrelated Causes.* The article, labeling the post from Mrs. Owens as "false" and a "hoax," exhibits an impressive amount of mental gymnastics in trying to debunk Mrs. Owens, going so far as to downplay the link between obesity and heart disease in one sentence, then boldly linking asthma with COVID-19 in the next.[6]

As an aside, this tactic of quibbling over very small semantic qualifiers instead of looking at the main point of a post is one of the most overused, obvious, and pedantic tools fact-checkers implement when trying to prove a weak point. The article by *Lead Stories* was the initial salvo in attempting to defame and deplatform Candace. By simply labeling the information Owens shared as false and a hoax, the attack on her character had begun.

Not one to be deterred, Candace continued digging for more information to help her and her followers better understand the strange world being created by the media in light of COVID-19. A few weeks after her initial post, on April 28, 2020, Owens published a post on her Facebook page that questioned the relationship between the counting of flu deaths and COVID-19 deaths in early 2020:

> According to CDC reports—2020 is working out to be the lowest flu death season of the decade. 20,000 flu deaths took place before Covid-19 in January, and then only 4,000 deaths thereafter. To give you context: 80,000 Americans died of the flu in 2019.[7]

The Second Facebook Post incorporated the text of a tweet published by Candace on her Twitter account:

> Possibly the greatest trade deal ever inked was between the flu virus and #coronavirus. So glad nobody is dying of the flu anymore, and therefore the CDC has abruptly decided to stop calculating flu deaths altogether. Agreements between viruses are the way of the future![8]

The purpose of Candace's Second Facebook Post was not to republish actual statistics but to raise an issue in an ongoing debate surrounding COVID-19. It reads more like a critique of the media's response to the ongoing pandemic and tries to highlight an issue in public perception. However, the fact-checkers, acting as the supreme arbiters of truth, keyed in on the dissenting nature of the information and upped the ante.

This time, *USA Today* flexed its fact-checking muscles on April 30, 2020, by creating an article and using it to directly label Candace's Second Facebook Post as false. How Facebook highlighted the fact-check stood in direct opposition to her ability to drive traffic to her site (a vital way she generated revenue through her Facebook presence) in two ways.

The first hurdle they introduced was the label itself. Most of Candace's 4.1 million users (other than those who voraciously followed and defended Owens) would be hesitant to engage with Candace's content any further. After all, few want to be associated with sharing "false" content to their networks. The stigma associated with a hoax label can reach far and wide, especially on social media.

The second barrier implemented on a fact-checked post was to cause the article created by *USA Today* to compete directly with click-through traffic from Facebook to her site or profile. Imagine if CNN went around directly linking its content to the content of NBC News—it's the digital version of ambulance chasing for lawyers. It not only takes traffic from Mrs. Owens, but it entices traffic toward *USA Today*— and with that purloined traffic comes the potential of a financial uptick for *USA Today*.

Even worse than having the articles written about her, and having them posted directly to the content she was sharing (often blurring the actual information Owens was sharing), the actions by *Lead Stories* and *USA Today* gave Facebook the fodder they needed. On June 22, 2020, Facebook demonetized Candace's Facebook account—suspending its ability to derive revenue from Facebook. To understand how devastating these events were to Candace when she was demonetized, it's estimated she was making an average of $35,500 per DAY through advertising revenue via Facebook. It's estimated that while Candace's account was demonetized due to fact-checking, she lost somewhere in the ballpark of $1.1 million.

One may ask what's so significant about this—after all, a celebrity personality like Mrs. Owens must have plenty of money. But you must remember that Candace Owens represents a business. While she is certainly the face and driving force, she has grown to be prolific and impactful in her appearances because she's not just some random person sitting behind a keyboard or an iPhone attached to a ring light, haphazardly popping off the first thing that comes to her mind whenever she pleases.

No, Mrs. Owens is much too responsible and intelligent for that. Every article, video, interview, and recorded conversation represents the culmination of countless hours of preparation, research, and strategic thought from not just herself but a team of thoughtful individuals that she supports through revenue. Just like your local restaurant would have to lay off servers, cooks, marketers, and bookkeepers if they experienced a rapid decline in revenue, the demonetization of Mrs. Owens on Facebook had a profound impact.

Welcome to Social Media Law—The Legislative Wild West

If you gain nothing else from this chapter, please understand this: When a social platform or a news agency attacks a personality by defaming and then demonetizing them, these entities are, in essence, completely taking away their ability to financially sustain themselves because they have lost access to their audience. When someone is demonetized, they are being deplatformed. And when their platform is taken away, their voice is being removed.

The natural follow-up question is usually something along the lines of, *How can these social media platforms just deplatform someone? Aren't they infringing on the First Amendment when they do so?*

We must realize that social media platforms are private companies and, therefore, not bound by the First Amendment, which only restricts government actions. These platforms have their own First Amendment rights, allowing them to moderate content on their websites without infringing on users' First Amendment rights. This is similar to legal cases involving businesses and their rights under the First Amendment.

The government cannot dictate how social media platforms moderate content. Attempts by various states to regulate this moderation have often failed due to First Amendment protections. Additionally, Section 230 of the

Federal Communications Decency Act protects most sites from being sued for the content posted by their users.

Section 230, enacted almost 30 years ago, is the legal foundation of the Internet. It protects internet platforms from being held liable for third-party content posted on their sites, with certain exceptions for content that is obscene, violent, harassing, or otherwise objectionable.

Examples of third-party content include reader comments on news websites, tweets on Twitter, posts on Facebook, photos on Instagram, and reviews on Yelp. For instance, if a Yelp reviewer posts something defamatory about a business, the business can sue the reviewer for libel but cannot sue Yelp due to Section 230. The law states: "No provider or user of an interactive computer service shall be treated as the publisher or speaker of any information provided by another information content provider."[9] This provision is often credited with enabling the growth of the Internet by allowing platforms to operate without constant fear of litigation. Furthermore, Section 230 allows these services to restrict access to content they find objectionable.

In summary, social media platforms have the authority to decide what content is acceptable and can choose to host or moderate content as they see fit. Therefore, arguments that suspensions or bans from these platforms violate free speech rights are not applicable. Section 230 serves as both a shield, protecting platforms from liability for user content, and a sword, allowing them to moderate that content.[10]

That tends to make sense—that is, until the day that these social media platforms are taken over by the government. Given some of the news about how information regarding COVID-19 was being influenced by frequent and pointed meetings between high-ranking government officials and representatives of Meta, Twitter, and Google, we may not be far from this reality. Then, we suddenly seem to be stuck in limbo between two opinions. These are private companies and, therefore, can't be made to act outside of their private use guidelines. However, they are not acting purely in a private capacity and, therefore, have responsibilities that seem to extend into the public sphere.

To try and address this dichotomy, there have been several major attempts to legally reclassify social media. To date, lawmakers have tried to draw comparisons between "common carriers," "public forums," and "public accommodations." If any of these three designations could be legally applied, the responsibilities of companies managing social platforms would alter drastically. However, as we will see, none of these approaches have been close to being successful.

Designating social media as a common carrier would mean that it is considered an essential good/service for all members of the public. This is similar to railroads or utilities. They would also be required to treat all users equally, as they effectively have monopoly-like power. But generally speaking, social media is free and is not a mere conduit like water or power. They provide screening, moderating, curating, fact-checking, and a whole other host of functions. Thus, the courts have rejected the comparison.

The next natural thought might be to consider social media platforms as public accommodations, akin to food, lodging, or entertainment. Given the nature of how they are consumed, this seems closer to a common carrier. They would then fall under such laws as the Federal Civil Rights Act of 1964[11] and would have to operate accordingly for all protected classes. But applying these laws to non-physical spaces is a dangerous game. There is no uniformity of opinion on how it might work.

Our last option would be to consider them a public forum. The concept of the open debate forum for public use is an old one, to be sure. With this designation, everyone would be protected, and nobody could be silenced. Literally, no viewpoint could be discriminated against. Many would agree that this is the best definition for social media, and would create the best results. But here again, we get stuck. The government alone can designate a public forum, and this can be very controversial, given that these spaces are in the hands of privately owned companies. It would take away the ability of a company to create a space with its own rules.[12]

Each of the three above arguments has certain elements of merit. But each also has elements that feel a bit like trying to jam a square peg into a round hole. None of the arguments fit just right. And until we're able to get new and comprehensive legislation for what social media has become, we're going to continue to live in a world of ambiguity where these corporations can simultaneously hide behind the First Amendment while acting as information overlords—censoring, controlling, labeling, and fact-checking users and content as they see fit.

Users, if they want to participate in the national and global conversations happening on these platforms, are left with two options. Obey the capricious rules—and ultimately conform to the censorship. Or fight. Candace chose to fight.

> I decided that I was not going to give up and sit down. The fact-checkers ... they're activists for the Left and shut down your speech if they don't like it.[13]

In October of 2020, I represented Candace as she filed suit against both *Lead Stories* and *USA Today*. Owens didn't land on the decision to pursue legal actions lightly. But after countless failed attempts to appeal the labeling of her content as "false" and a "hoax," which led to Facebook demonetizing her, she honestly had no choice. Hers wasn't a battle just for herself. It was a battle on behalf of any user who may find themselves swimming against the ideological currents controlled by corporations with a personal agenda.

Two years later, in October of 2022, our final appeal to the Supreme Court was rejected without comment. In every ruling leading to that decision, first initially, then in our appeal in Delaware, the judges did not feel there was an actionable claim based on the law as it stands. I will discuss in a later chapter how the politics of the justices involved in cases like these may have had an impact on their rulings. Still, ultimately, the ambiguity of the laws around both defamation and social media made the case more difficult than it should have been.

Ambiguity—Defamation's Closest Friend

As we consider how the media acts to silence dissenting voices, which have grown powerful enough to snatch even a little influence from them, we need to understand the power they gain from the ambiguity brought about by the breakneck pace at which the digital space is developing. When I reflect on how different the world looks compared to when I was a child, it's easy to dip into nostalgia. We smile at dinner parties and say things like, *To think about all of the phone numbers I used to have memorized…now I'm not sure I can tell you my spouse's number without looking at my phone,* or *How did we settle arguments before phones?* Now, you just look up the right answer. But rapid changes like we're experiencing breed confusion.

As an example of this confusion, let's briefly analyze the way *Lead Stories* articulates how they participate in Facebook's fact-checking process:

> The company works to mitigate the dissemination of false information across the Facebook platform through its fact-checking service, for which it receives compensation from Facebook. However, Lead Stories emphasizes that Facebook does not influence which content it chooses to fact-check or the outcomes of those fact-checks. The process of selecting content for review is based on Lead Stories' independent decisions, utilizing Facebook's tools designed for fact-checkers, which flag potentially false content identified by Facebook's systems or users.[14]

In the second sentence, *Lead Stories* is quick to point out that Facebook does not influence which content they choose to fact-check. However, in the very next sentence, they clearly state that they use tools that Facebook has designed for fact-checkers—tools that flag potential false content identified by

Facebook's system or users. So, which is it? Is *Lead Stories* completely autonomous regarding the content they fact-check, or are they directed where to look based on Facebook's fact-checking tools? It gets worse.

In deciding which posts to examine, Lead Stories prioritizes those related to current events and assesses several criteria, including the post's checkability (excluding pure opinions, predictions, or vague statements), potential harm, likelihood of going viral, relevance to U.S. audiences, and more. Lead Stories follows a comprehensive methodology to investigate the truthfulness of selected posts, considering factors like the origin of the claim, available evidence, presence of inconsistencies, and the credibility of sources, among others.

Upon concluding an investigation, Lead Stories publishes an article reflecting its findings and notifies Facebook of its decision through a designated portal, allowing Facebook to take appropriate action on the flagged content. This may include reducing the distribution of content deemed false or altered and affecting the abilities of users to monetize and advertise. Facebook outlines a process for disputing fact-check ratings, offering content creators the opportunity to appeal directly to the third-party fact-checking partner, with the potential for reversing content demotions and other penalties if the rating is changed upon review.[15]

Again, they reference the final article they publish and how they notify Facebook so that Facebook can take appropriate action on the flagged post. If they had no idea what content to fact-check and are acting 100% independently, then how do their articles magically match the content that Facebook flagged? And what's the recourse for the user who has been fact-checked? They have to figure out how to reach out to the third-party fact-checker so they can address something that happened to them on Facebook.

It is a well-constructed and self-reinforcing labyrinth designed to protect itself and make battling for one's good name nearly impossible.

This is just one example of dozens that we could analyze in light of what many consider a deliberate attempt to add confusion to a landscape that is already difficult enough to manage. Each finger points to another entity, and as people like Candace try to wind their way through the various twists and turns, the corporations are banking on the premise that these influencers are losing followers with each passing day.

These are the tactics that I mentioned at the start of this chapter. When someone has too much influence (and has proven to be unmanageable by those who seek to own the narrative), they start their assault by slapping a label on the dissenter. Often, this serves to reduce the personality's followers and diminishes the reach of their content. If there's pushback—if the rebel persists—then confusion is employed.

Confusion can come in the form of fact-checkers dissecting tiny, often contrived, discrepancies in a statement for the sake of being able to label something as false or misleading. The confusion grows when corporations hide behind ambiguous laws and overly complex systems of fact-checking subcontractors and appeal processes. All this leads to a populace that is left fending for themselves, while the rebellious personality tries to dig their way out from under wrongful labels, laborious appeal processes, and lengthy legal battles.

Ultimately, if they can make a label stick, if they can prominently display a link to a defamatory article in a way that deters further engagement with the personality's additional content, and if they can choose to demonetize any advertising on their platform, they are inches away from achieving their goal of silencing an unruly voice. It's a rare breed that can survive an onslaught like that.

I'm happy to confirm that Candace has not only survived; she is thriving. And that's a good thing for the national conversation. Others have not been so lucky.

But these corporations aren't done. If silencing through deplatforming isn't possible, they will take yet another heinous step. And we're seeing it play out before us as we head into the 2024 presidential election.

Chapter Notes

1 Deadspin. "Sinclair's Soldiers in Trump's War on Media", YouTube Video, 2018, 1:38, https://www.youtube.com/watch?v=_fHfgU8oMSo.

2 "About Blexit," Blexit, accessed May 24, 2024, https://www.blexit.com/about.

3 Candace Owens, "Important Information for Everyone to Know About…," Meta (Facebook), March 29, 2020, 2020, https://www.facebook.com/realCandaceOwens/posts/3598900840181091.

4 Facebook, "Understanding Meta's Fact-Checking Program," 2023, accessed May 24, 2024, https://www.facebook.com/government-nonprofits/blog/misinformation-resources.

5 Robert Schmad, "Fact Check: Nearly 100 Percent of Political Contributions from Fact Checkers Go to Democrats," last modified Jun 13, 2023, 2023, accessed May 24, 2024, https://freebeacon.com/media/fact-check-nearly-100-percent-of-political-contributions-from-fact-checkers-go-to-democrats/.

6 Ryan Cooper, "Fact Check: Covid-19 Not Being Blamed for Deaths Primarily Due to Unrelated Causes," last modified Apr 1, 2020, 2020, accessed May 24, 2024, https://leadstories.com/hoax-alert/2020/04/Fact-Check-COVID19-NOT-Being-Blamed-For-Deaths-Primarily-Due-To-Unrelated-Causes.html.

7 Candace Owens, "According to Cdc Reports…," Meta (Facebook)2020, https://www.facebook.com/realCandaceOwens/photos/according-to-cdc-reports-2020-is-working-out-to-be-the-lowest-flu-death-season-o/3701927883211719/.

8 Candace Owens (@RealCandaceO), "Possibly the Greatest Trade Deal Ever…," X (Twitter), Apr 28, 2020, 2020, https://twitter.com/RealCandaceO/status/1255138389080203267.

9 Communications Decency Act of 1996

10 Sara Morrison, "Section 230, the Internet Law the Supreme Court Could Change, Explained," Maverick Studios, last modified February 23, 2023, 2020, accessed May 24, 2024, https://maverickstudios.net/2023/02/23/section-230-the-internet-law-the-supreme-court-could-change-explained/.

11 Civil Rights Act of 1964; 7/2/1964; Enrolled Acts and Resolutions of Congress, 1789 - 2011; General Records of the United States Government, Record Group 11; National Archives Building, Washington, DC.

12 Kevin Goldberg, "Perspective: Why Arguments for Regulating Social Media Fail the First Amendment Test," Freedom Forum, accessed May 2024, 2024, https://www.freedomforum.org/social-media-regulation-first-amendment/.

13 Candace Owens (@RealCandaceO), "Guess What?!," X (Twitter), Nov 5, 2020, 2020, https://x.com/RealCandaceO/status/1324515021657812992.

14 Owens, et al. v. Lead Stories, LLC, et al.

15 Owens

LAW IS A BATTLEFIELD

THE WEAPONIZATION OF "JUSTICE"

*"Nobody is truly canceled unless they consent to it
and they willingly play their assigned roles"*
- Matt Walsh

In October of 2022, popular conservative commentator Matt Walsh posted a YouTube video where he detailed how the progressive Left had been attacking him for his views on gender, sexuality, family, and various other hot-button topics. In a fiery crescendo, he summarily refused to "bend the knee" to cancel culture and famously stated, "Nobody is truly canceled unless they consent to it and they willingly play their assigned roles."[1]

It was his version of a rallying cry, in essence calling his viewers to never give up, never apologize for one's ideals, and certainly never cave to the pressures that can come crashing down hard due to the hit jobs, deplatforming, lies, and defamation that come from cancel culture.

In a subsequent interview, Ben Shapiro (host of the Ben Shapiro Show, co-founder and editor emeritus of *The Daily Wire*, among other prominent roles) demonstrated solidarity with Walsh by saying that *The Daily Wire* "had his back"[2] and would never fire him for stating his deeply held beliefs. It was a rare moment where a company firmly stood strong, refused to walk back a viewpoint, and defiantly told their viewers, advertisers, and everyone else that even if they lost revenue, they would stay true to their ideals. If only we could all work for a company bold enough to stand by us when the mob grabs their pitchforks and begins lighting their torches.

Walsh continues to be attacked to this day. He's had his email and phone hacked, had personal details shared publicly, been threatened with violence, demonetized by YouTube, and doxxed countless times. In short, he's experienced everything I've outlined in the previous two chapters. But what happens when all of those tactics aren't enough to silence a person?

In the rarest of instances, a figure can rise to a level of prominence well beyond Candace Owens or Matt Walsh, whom the media and political progressives consider so heinous they will stop at nothing to see them destroyed. We are seeing this dynamic playing out in front of us in real-time in the case of Donald Trump.

We cannot go more than two minutes in the daily news cycle without seeing Donald Trump. Traditional and social media outlets seem to share a massive obsession with this man. His polarizing personality has become a benchmark for how people are defined politically, and many topics are viewed in their relationship to his policies and stated beliefs. Let me be clear—I'm not what you'd consider to be a "Trump guy," and I'd never describe myself as "MAGA." But I support President Trump, focus on his policies, and mostly agree with what he did as president. Personally, as more of a religious conservative, I have tried to steer clear of the association—but I find it amazing that I even need to qualify this.

Sadly, I think the need to clarify my position speaks to how divided we've become, largely due to how the media has succeeded in polarizing us around this man.

But when I apply the lens of media hit jobs, and how large companies with extreme ideologies are willing to deplatform those with whom they disagree, I can't help but take notice of how Mr. Trump is being treated. He has exposed what lengths the media and political rivals are willing to go to in an effort to silence and intimidate someone—mainly because none of it seems to be working with him. The media tried the standard hit job (as we discussed in Chapter five), and it went nowhere. They attempted to deplatform him (as we discussed in Chapter six), and he instead made his own platform.

So they had to become even more extreme, and in doing so, they revealed what they would do to anyone they could not cancel or silence.

To best understand what we're dealing with now, it's helpful to consider how we got to this unprecedented state where we're watching multiple indictments (carrying dozens of charges) being brought against the former president.

Trump's Rise and Fall—A Snapshot

Donald Trump has been a prominent figure in the media for decades, first as a real estate mogul and reality TV star, and then as a political figure. He was celebrated on both sides of the aisle, and even the media (albeit with a little bit of mixed reaction) seemed favorable to him in the early months of his campaign as he approached the election. But then the impossible happened, and Trump was elected.

To make matters worse, in response to criticism in the media, he started using the term "fake news" on December 10, 2016.[3] This marked the beginning of his frequent use of the phrase to describe and dismiss media outlets, along with their often outlandish reports that he disagreed with, or that portrayed him negatively.

It did not help that the search term "fake news" experienced an explosion in popularity (as reflected by Google Trends). This phrase still maintains about twice as much use as it did prior to him popularizing it.[4]

The love affair was over—Trump's political approach stood in stark contrast to the way politicians had danced alongside the media in a sort of sick symbiotic relationship. There were no carefully chosen words, and very few of his statements came through the outdated backchannels from the White House to the press corps. Most of what Trump said was directly to the citizens through Twitter posts full of biting quips, aggressive nicknames for his opponents, and terse rebukes of the media. This was a bridge too far, and it challenged the authority that so many mega conglomerates had enjoyed for so long—authority so powerful that it had been dictating how the Leader of the Free World should and should not act toward them.

Their response was to target Mr. Trump with an unending onslaught of hit jobs, deplatforming, and cancellation attempts. Most people could not financially (much less emotionally and psychologically) survive the brutality of the assaults leveled against him. But, in doing so, he shows that anyone unwilling to go along with the modern-day narrative will be attacked relentlessly. Trump's resilience against the established hit job playbook has led us to a cancel culture endgame. The attacks have penetrated from the public sphere into the legal world.

This seismic shift has turned Trump into the single largest case study of tactics employed by the media to date. Here is a brief review of what he has experienced since daring to oppose entrenched politicians, the media, and certain corporations. Note that I say "brief," because a complete listing and description would take up several chapters.

Phase I—The Hit Jobs

- Trump's First Impeachment (December 2019), in which he was charged with abuse of power and obstruction of Congress. He was later acquitted.[5]

- First presidential term—A litany of accusers come out against Trump, accusing him of sexual misconduct.[6]

- Trump's Second Impeachment (January 2021), where he was charged with insurrection and was acquitted again.[7]

Phase II—The Battle to Deplatform & Cut Off Support

- Facebook indefinitely suspended Trump on January 7, 2021.[8]

- Twitter permanently suspended Trump's account on January 8, 2021.[9]

- YouTube suspended Trump's account on January 12, 2021.[10]

- Gettr is launched and allows Trump a profile on July 4, 2021.[11]

- Rudy Giuliani was suspended from practicing law in New York on June 24, 2021.[12] Following this suspension, the District of Columbia's highest court also suspended Giuliani from practicing law in Washington, D.C., on July 7, 2021.[13]

- Trump launched Truth Social on Feb 21, 2022.[14]

- Peter Navarro, American economist who served in the Trump administration, was indicted on June 3, 2022.[15]

- Elon Musk completed his acquisition of Twitter on October 27, 2022.

- Musk reinstated Trump's Twitter account on November 19, 2022, after conducting a poll via a tweet to decide on the reinstatement.[16]

Phase III—Trump's Second Candidacy

- Trump announces his second candidacy on November 16, 2022, after years of failed cancellation and deplatforming attempts. The machine goes into full swing with legal retribution.[17]

- November 18, 2022: Attorney General Merrick Garland appoints Jack Smith as special counsel overseeing federal investigations into Trump.[18]

- March 30, 2023: Trump is indicted in New York on 34 counts of falsifying business records related to hush money payments.[19]

- June 8, 2023: A federal grand jury in Florida indicts Trump on 37 charges related to the mishandling of classified documents.[20]

- August 1, 2023: Trump is indicted in Washington, D.C., on charges related to his alleged efforts to overturn the 2020 presidential election.[21]

- August 14, 2023: A Georgia indictment charges Trump with 13 criminal counts related to interference in the 2020 election.

- January 2024: MSNBC (represented by Rachel Maddow) refuses to air Trump's Iowa victory speech, claiming that airing his "misinformation" would harm their journalistic integrity.[22]

- March 14, 2024: Trump attends a hearing regarding his suits, filed by his legal team.[23]

- April 15, 2024: The trial for the New York indictment begins.[24]

- May 20, 2024: The trial for the federal classified documents case is scheduled to begin.[25]

Lawfare—The Final Frontier of Cancel Culture

Regardless of how you feel about Mr. Trump, I think any individual with a discerning eye can see that the list above represents much more than your typical dealings with a politician. I don't need to go into the imbalance between the fervor demonstrated by both the media and the FBI when it came to how Mr. Trump handled some presidential documents after his time in office, compared to the blind eye and refusal to consider similar scrutiny for President Biden's handling of documents from his time as Vice President. And that's just one example of many.

Again, this isn't a Trump-defense chapter. I'm merely attempting to point out the imbalance—it's the same tactic that the media used when they purposely chose not to interview Nick Sandmann, and instead gave full exposure to Nathan Phillips and his exaggerated falsehoods. What's being done to Mr. Trump is on a much larger scale, and it's involving the entire justice system in the process.

As can be observed in the timeline, Trump is not the only one to feel the wrath of the near-religious fervor that has overtaken the country. Probably the scariest (and most notable) efforts are those of The 65 Project, which has been brilliantly compared to McCarthy-era tactics by Alan Dershowitz in his book *Get Trump*. The 65 Project's mission statement is clear:

> In the immediate aftermath of the 2020 election, Trump-allied lawyers filed 65 lawsuits across the country to overturn the legitimate election results. Finding the assertions bogus and riddled with false

statements, Republican- and Democratic-appointed judges uniformly dismissed the lawsuits. But success in the courtroom was not the only objective. Instead, the lawyers bringing these claims knew they were a key component of a larger effort to discredit the 2020 presidential election – and all future elections in which their preferred candidate lost.

The 65 Project is a bi-partisan effort to protect democracy and preserve the rule of law by deterring future attacks on our electoral system. We are holding accountable Big Lie Lawyers who bring fraudulent and malicious lawsuits to overturn legitimate election results, and working with bar associations to revitalize the disciplinary process so that lawyers, including public officials, who subvert democracy will be punished.

Lawyers take an oath to stand as officers of the court, bound by a code of conduct and ethical requirements that do not apply to the public more broadly. They cannot uphold that duty while lying to the court or the public about the factual grounds for phony claims. The 65 Project will work to hold accountable the lawyers who raise fraudulent claims to overturn legitimate election results while also creating a rule-based system to prevent future attempts and to strengthen the mechanisms for accountability and deterrence.[26]

Or, to put it more bluntly and honestly (as one anonymous source associated with the group did with *rawstory.com*):

> This is mostly important for the deterrent effect that it can bring so that you can kill the pool of available legal talent going forward[27]

Readers who have studied the previous chapters on hit jobs and deplatforming will recognize one familiar tactic within The 65 Project's description. The *Righteous Victim* plays a prominent role in The Project's diatribe about the moral and ethical responsibility they feel in holding those they have aligned themselves against accountable. Instead of identifying their actions as "retaliatory" or "overreaching" (two words that could easily be used), they instead present themselves as valiant rebels, standing in the face of a tyrant.

Last I checked, President Trump wasn't using the full extent of the justice system to punish his rivals. I think these folks, if they woke up in the Star Wars universe, would find themselves more closely aligned with Darth Vader than Han Solo.

It is worth noting that this application of lawfare is so far out in the open, that some of the very people leading the charge in prosecuting Mr. Trump are in their roles in order to do precisely that. Most notably, Letitia James, the New York State Attorney General, has had Mr. Trump in her sights since at least 2018, when she vowed to shine a "bright light into every dark corner of his real estate dealings,"[28] while calling him a conman and an illegitimate president. Apparently, *innocent until proven guilty* isn't as important for attorney generals to consider as it used to be.

Not to be outdone, Judge Engoron, who presides over the same trial that Ms. James is prosecuting, had a Judicial Ethics Complaint filed against him by Rep. Elise Stefanik based on Judge Engoron's comments about Mr. Trump. In her letter, Rep. Stefanik said:

> Simply put, Judge Engoron has displayed a clear judicial bias against the defendant throughout the case, breaking several rules in the New York Code of Judicial Conduct. Last year, Judge Engoron told President Trump's attorney that the former president is "just a bad guy" who Democrat New York Attorney General Letitia James "should go after as the chief law enforcement officer of the state."[29]

Despite his clear bias against Mr. Trump, Judge Engoron would not recuse himself—something countless justices have done on a regular basis for far less. In my view, this statement creates the appearance of impropriety, since this is the standard judges use to decide if they should recuse themselves from a particular case. Most certainly, Americans expect that a judge presiding over such a controversial trial should appear entirely impartial. That was not the case with Judge Engoron.

And when Justice Egoron offered his ruling, which requires Mr. Trump to pay $464 million or face having his assets seized by Ms. James, those in the prosecutorial community were gobsmacked. Many legal experts saw the amount to be so exorbitant that many are saying Mr. Trump has a clear appeal based on the Eighth Amendment—you know, the one that offers citizens protection against cruel and unusual punishment.

In an interview with Fox News Digital, a former U.S. attorney in Atlanta, GA, said,

> "It is unheard of to seek repayment of over $464 million when there was no identifiable victim and when the entities on the other side of all of these transactions were sophisticated investors who conducted their own due diligence."[30]

Even more shocking is that Justice Egoron's ruling saw the steep price as a fair righting of a wrong against the banks whose executives testified in this trial that they would, and have, continued to do business with Mr. Trump. Maybe Justice Egoron was distracted by the courtroom cameras during the testimony of the bank executives.

Honestly, if the law weren't being abused so insidiously, the extreme actions taken against Mr. Trump (all for the sake of punishing him for not bending the knee) would seem like an ironic write-up from a parody news site like the *Babylon Bee*. Instead, I fear our justice system is being turned into a real-time example of protesting a little *too* much.

The Final Straw

If you think what's happening to Mr. Trump is isolated due to how polarizing a figure Mr. Trump tends to be, you are wrong. In future chapters, I will talk about the precedent-setting power that comes with each and every defamation trial.

Friends, the scale of this attack cannot go unnoticed. It's one thing for corporations to hide behind overly complex and poorly explained processes that insulate them from acting in good faith. It's a very different thing to take a defamatory attack to the level it's being brought against Mr. Trump.

I have to imagine that when an Allied pilot in the Second World War first came into contact with a never-before-seen German jet-powered fighter aircraft, the world must have stopped. And in that terrifying moment, the Allied pilot likely understood the world would never be the same. The rules of combat would need to change, and for the sake of the free world, the Allies would need to do something to catch up. When the judicial system of the United States of America is being manipulated in such a way that it's becoming the next leg of the stool on which defamation can comfortably sit, we find ourselves staring at an enemy with superior technology.

If Mr. Trump's opponents can get some of these charges to stick, it would undoubtedly be a boon for them. So far, they have been largely unsuccessful. Equally as desirable, if they can litigate him into financial ruin through the continued imposition of legal fees and crushing fines, then his ability to run a successful presidential campaign will end. If they can keep him distracted and in courtrooms while they throw charge after charge at the wall, well, that's valuable time that he's not on the campaign trail pointing out their hypocrisy and building his influence despite their best efforts. Just like Mr. Sandmann and Mrs. Owens, they want Trump's silence —and they will go as far as attempting to put him in jail to gain it.

We are crossing the Rubicon in more ways than one. If this new addition to the defamation playbook proves successful, we will see it employed more and more; we will see more people being punished for not complying with the capricious desires of the media and over-zealous politicians.

Chapter Notes

1 Math Walsh. "Matt Walsh's Apology to the Left", Oct 6, 2022, YouTube Video, 2022, 15:21, https://www.youtube.com/watch?v=WGW0o0fj7uk.

2 Triggernometry. "An Honest Conversation with Ben Shapiro", YouTube Video, 2023, 1:04:00, https://www.youtube.com/watch?v=HM282oySNbM.

3 Haley Britzky, "Everything Trump Has Called "Fake News"," last modified Jul 9, 2017, 2017, accessed May 24, 2024, https://www.axios.com/2017/12/15/everything-trump-has-called-fake-news-1513303959.

4 Results available at https://trends.google.com/trends/explore?date=2016-01-01%202024-04-27&geo=US&q=fake%20news&hl=en

5 Andrew Desiderio Kyle Cheney, and John Bresnahan, "Trump Acquitted on Impeachment Charges, Ending Gravest Threat to His Presidency," Politico, last modified February 5, 2020, 2020, accessed May 2024, 2024, https://www.politico.com/news/2020/02/05/trump-impeachment-vote-110805.

6 Meghan Keneally, "List of Trump's Accusers and Their Allegations of Sexual Misconduct," last modified Sep 18, 2020, 2020, accessed May 24, 2024, https://abcnews.go.com/Politics/list-trumps-accusers-allegations-sexual-misconduct/story?id=51956410.

7 Lisa Mascaro et al., "Trump Impeached after Capitol Riot in Historic Second Charge," last modified Jan 13, 2021, 2021, accessed May 24, 2024, https://apnews.com/article/trump-impeachment-vote-capitol-siege-0a6f2a348a6e43f27d5e1dc486027860.

8 Will Oremus, "Tech Giants Banned Trump. But Did They Censor Him?," last modified Jan 7, 2022, 2022, accessed May 24, 2024, https://www.washingtonpost.com/technology/2022/01/07/trump-facebook-ban-censorship/.

9 Oremus

10 Oremus

11 Liam Cole, "Former Trump Spokesman Launches New Social Media Platform Gettr," News Nation USA, 2021, accessed May 24, 2024, https://web.archive.org/web/20211021192931/https://newsnationusa.com/uncategorized/former-trump-spokesman-launches-new-social-media-platform-gettr/.

12 Jim Mustian, "New York Court Suspends Rudy Giuliani's Law License," last modified June 24, 2021, 2021, accessed May 24, 2024, https://apnews.com/article/rudy-giuliani-new-york-law-license-suspended-c67f4504a22f8642d6096f29e3a5c51e.

13 Rachel Weiner, "Rudy Giuliani Suspended from Practicing Law in D.C. Court," last modified Jul 7, 2021, 2021, accessed May 24, 2024, https://www.washingtonpost.com/local/legal-issues/giuliani-washington-court/2021/07/07/9f7a7f5c-df6a-11eb-9f54-7eee10b5fcd2_story.html.

14 Dan Whitcomb, "Former U.S. President Donald Trump Launches 'Truth' Social Media Platform," last modified April 30, 2024, 2021, accessed May 24, 2024, https://www.reuters.com/world/us/former-us-president-donald-trump-launches-new-social-media-platform-2021-10-21/.

15 "Peter Navarro Indicted for Contempt of Congress," United States Attorney's Office (District of Columbia), last modified June 3, 2022, 2022, accessed May 24, 2024, https://www.justice.gov/usao-dc/pr/peter-navarro-indicted-contempt-congress.

16 Matt G. Southern, "Elon Musk's Twitter Takeover: A Timeline of Events," last modified Nov 16, 2022, 2022, accessed May 24, 2024, https://www.searchenginejournal.com/elon-musks-twitter-takeover-a-timeline-of-events/470927/.

17 Gabby Orr, Kristen Holmes, and Veronica Stracqualursi, "Former President Donald Trump Announces a White House Bid for 2024," last modified Nov 16, 2022, 2022, accessed May 24, 2024, https://www.cnn.com/2022/11/15/politics/trump-2024-presidential-bid/index.html.

18 Jacob Fischler, "Updated: The Trump Indictments: A Seven-Year Timeline of Key Developments," last modified May 14, 2024, 2023, accessed May 24, 2024, https://penncapital-star.com/campaigns-elections/updated-the-trump-indictments-a-seven-year-timeline-of-key-developments/.

19 Melissa Wuinn, and Graham Kates, "Trump's 4 Indictments in Detail: A Quick-Look Guide to Charges, Trial Dates and Key Players for Each Case," last modified May 9, 2024, 2024, accessed May 24, 2024, https://www.cbsnews.com/news/trump-indictments-details-guide-charges-trial-dates-people-case/.

20 Fischler

21 John Santucci Katherine Faulders, Lucien Bruggeman, and Alexander Mallin, "Trump Hit with Sweeping Indictment in Alleged Effort to Overturn 2020 Election," ABC News, 2023, accessed May 2024, 2024, https://abcnews.go.com/US/trump-indicted-charges-related-efforts-overturn-2020-election/story?id=101612810.

22 Christopher Wiggins, "Msnbc's Decision Not to Air Trump's Iowa Victory Speech Live Ignites Right-Wing Firestorm," last modified Jan 17, 2024, 2024, accessed May 24, 2024, https://www.advocate.com/media/rachel-maddow-trump-iowa-speech.

23 Wiggins

24 Wiggins

25 Wiggins

26 "About Us," The 65 Project, 2023, accessed May 24, 2024, https://the65project.com/about/.

27 Travis Gettys, "'Threatening Their Livelihood': Democrats Target Pro-Trump Attorneys for Disbarment," last modified Mar 7, 2022, 2022, accessed May 24, 2024, https://www.rawstory.com/the-65-project/.

28 Anthony Izaguirre, "Ny Attorney General Letitia James Has a Long History of Fighting Trump and Other Powerful Targets," last modified Sept 28, 2023, 2023, accessed May 24, 2024, https://www.usnews.com/news/politics/articles/2023-09-28/ny-attorney-general-letitia-james-has-a-long-history-of-fighting-trump-other-powerful-targets.

29 Katherine Doyle, "Icymi: Nbc News – Rep. Elise Stefanik Files Ethics Complaint against Judge in Trump's Civil Fraud Trial," 2023, accessed May 24, 2024, https://eliseforcongress.com/2023/11/10/icymi-nbc-news-rep-elise-stefanik-files-ethics-complaint-against-judge-in-trumps-civil-fraud-trial/.

30 Brianna Herlihy, "Legal Experts Say Trump's Whopping New York Fee Could Be 'Excessive' under Constitution: 'Unheard Of'," last modified Mar 26, 2024, 2024, accessed May 24, 2024, https://www.foxnews.com/politics/legal-experts-say-trumps-whopping-new-york-fee-could-be-excessive-under-constitution-unheard-of.

REMOVING THE BLINDFOLD OF JUSTICE

WHEN JUDGES GET POLITICAL

"I think the independence of our federal judiciary is one of our nation's hallmark and pride. Judges can't defend themselves. They depend on members of the bar and the public to help preserve that institution."
- Ruth Bader Ginsburg

I often tell my children that the world in which we live has absolutely nothing in common with the world in which I grew up. Sure, the streets still have the same names, and cars still travel up and down them, but the spirit of things is not recognizable. To me, there used to be a United States that we could all agree we cared for and respected. That love of country was shared by the vast majority of Americans. Even the dissenters did not hate the country. They did not hate their culture. They did not hate themselves.

But over the past fifty years, as the nation has changed in ways we have all experienced, it seems as if we no longer agree upon what our country should be, or what it means to love our country. At least, that is how I feel about things. You might say, *Todd, that's a bit hyperbolic, don't you think?* It's not. In fact, the United States has become increasingly divided, and that shows up everywhere, including in our court system. Our system was designed nearly 250 years ago by brilliant men who looked at other systems and tried to create one that would promote human flourishing and last for centuries.

When establishing the judicial branch of our government, I believe our Founding Fathers created something remarkable in its ability to ensure that justice was not tied to politics. However, as we've seen over the past fifty years, their creation is under assault. As the political divide increases, we are electing more polarized officials, and, in turn, these officials have begun to appoint people to the judiciary who seem to be more interested in advocacy than adjudicating. As this fervor increases, both sides of the political aisle believe the other has lost its way. The courts, by extension, have become more divided and partisan than ever.

Let us begin by examining how the United States developed its court system. At its founding, three of our Founding Fathers, Alexander Hamilton, James Madison, and John Jay, authored *The Federalist Papers*.

Alexander Hamilton, in *The Federalist # 78*, famously noted that the federal courts "were designed to be an intermediate body between the people and their legislature," with the intent that they would safeguard against representatives acting outside the authority granted by the Constitution.[1]

Hamilton argued for the creation of an independent third branch of government—a Supreme Court—which would not be subject to either legislative or executive power. In Britain, Hamilton noted, the courts were subject to the control of the legislature. However, because he believed in the wisdom of the people, he wanted something different, something to protect the people from the whims of the legislature—a necessary departure from what he'd experienced in Britain. He wrote that "in no case" should the Supreme Court "ABOLISH the trial by jury."[2]

Thus, our Founding Fathers established an immensely powerful judiciary, separate from the executive and legislative branches, with an important limit on its power—it could not limit a person's right to a trial by jury.

As a quick aside, I recommend that you read some of *The Federalist Papers*. I am by no means a legal scholar, but reading someone like Alexander Hamilton write about the formation of our government sends chills down your spine. Hamilton's and other Federalists' writings are incredibly insightful, and more relevant than ever. I wish we could bring our Founding Fathers back to guide us today.

The obvious chasm that separates the quality of leadership today from what we had with our Founding Fathers is profound. Imagine a world run by brilliant and ethical leaders like George Washington and Alexander Hamilton versus the political class we have today, comprised of so many attention-seeking narcissists.

Alexander Hamilton and the Founding Fathers created Article III of the Constitution and the judicial branch. As we know from decades of commentary about the judicial branch, Congress has the power to appoint federal judges. It also created the lower federal courts. The District Courts are the federal trial courts. There are also intermediate courts of appeal below the Supreme Court known as the Circuit Courts.

At the top of the judicial pyramid is the Supreme Court. This is the Court designed to have immense power to shape society and set the course of the entire Nation. And it has done so repeatedly.

Each ruling by the Supreme Court has the potential to shape the way certain rights and privileges are enforced and interpreted. In Chapter 11 of this book, I discuss how many landmark cases like *Brown v. Board of Education*, *New York Times v. Sullivan*, and *Roe v. Wade* have literally impacted the daily lives of millions of people over decades.

These decisions on race, personal identity, and the right of women to choose whether or not to terminate their own pregnancy are massive pronouncements on who we are as a nation. They have united us in condemning the national stain of slavery and race discrimination, but have divided us regarding the sanctity of marriage and the sanctity of a person's body.

Each of these decisions was a pronouncement and mandate of who we had to be. We had no choice. These decisions were not made as a people, but instead by a Court. Nine people told tens of millions who they had to be. That is immense power. And, surprisingly, we have put up with it.

I know the types of lawyers who are chosen to serve on the Supreme Court. These are the most brilliant people on the planet. Each is incredibly educated and masterful. Each is as deserving as a person could be to pass judgment on the many challenging issues we face. But not one of them is without sin, without ambition, and without flaws. That is why when they make decisions that offend tens of millions of people, the people lose faith in their impartiality—they believe they are political actors with an agenda against what they want. Be it individuals who support abortion or oppose it, each side has become increasingly distrustful of a Court whose decisions have the power to shape the identity of our nation.

It is not an exaggeration to say the Supreme Court has played an outsized role in society. This is especially true over the past 25 years, during which we have seen our governmental leaders fail repeatedly. They failed in the Gulf War, they failed in the Great Financial Crisis of 2008, they failed with COVID-19, they failed in Afghanistan, and now they are failing on immigration and fiscal responsibility. So, as two of the three branches of government crash and burn, we are left to rely on the judiciary. But even this powerful Court may not be able to save us, especially when many people perceive judges at the federal, state, and local levels to be highly political and unreliable.

The source of this discontent, I believe, is because appointments to the federal bench are lifetime appointments, which supposedly give federal judges the freedom to ignore politics when making decisions. But like anything, judges make decisions shaped by their life experiences and political philosophy. That was as true in our past as it is today.

I was a history major in college and have read dozens of books on U.S. history. I have studied our Constitution, the Revolution, the Civil War, World War II, and all aspects of politics in our nearly 250-year history. I have three photos of Abraham Lincoln in my office! This foundation of knowledge has informed my daily reading of multiple newspapers over the last 40 years. My education and work as a lawyer are the cornerstones upon which I base my views of the judiciary.

I think the judiciary is, and always has been, shaped by the politics of the time. It is inherently political—some would say, "politicized." But today, we do not have Washington and Hamilton running things; we have Joe Biden and Donald Trump. We have Alexandria Ocasio Cortez and Matt Gaetz. One side hates the other. We also have a judiciary shaped by our times. It is one that thinks a lot about ethnicity, class, education, and sexual orientation. U.S. Supreme Court Justice Sonia Sotomayor is an example of a justice whose life experiences dominate her thinking.

By all accounts, Justice Sotomayor is a highly qualified and brilliant judge. But like all of us, she has been formed by her lived experiences. She once wrote that she "would hope that a wise Latina woman with the richness of her experiences would more often than not reach a better conclusion than a white male who hasn't lived that life."[3] I guess being raised in the Bronx by your Puerto Rican mother somehow makes a person a better decision-maker. What does this philosophy say about one of the most powerful decision-makers in the world? It says she looks inwardly to her personal life experiences as the foundation of how she makes decisions.

I contrast this with the Founding Fathers, who did not look at themselves as the point of decision, but relied upon the wisdom of the ages to guide their decisions. I cannot imagine Alexander Hamilton, whom John Adams called the "bastard brat of a Scottish peddler,"[4] ever feeling victimized because he was illegitimate (what does that even mean today?), or because he grew up in the West Indies under challenging circumstances.

Instead of relying upon the challenges of his youth as formative and determinative of his character, he instead overcame these challenges to become one of the most singularly brilliant people ever to live. He changed the world by helping to create the United States. He never wrote about the wisdom he gained in the West Indies or what it meant to be considered a bastard. Instead, he wrote about other forms of government and how we could improve upon them. This was not a personal perspective, but a global perspective.

The distinction between Alexander Hamilton and Justice Sotomayor is truly the distinction that plagues us today. While Hamilton was a fierce competitor and an ambitious politician (as we can see from his writing in *The Federalist Papers*), his work was based upon the cold, hard analysis of nations that came before, which informed decisions regarding how to construct a government that would last. He wanted a stable government that would promote human flourishing. The political and philosophical works the Founding Fathers relied upon were written by classical politicians and philosophers, such as the ancient Greek philosopher Aristotle and the Roman politician Cicero. The Founding Fathers also relied upon more contemporary philosophers of the Enlightenment.[5]

We Have Wandered From the Original Vision

So, without trying to cover a semester or two of college philosophy, why is it significant that the Founding Fathers drew upon the wisdom of the Greeks and Romans up to their era of the Enlightenment for guidance? To me, it means they tried to create a system where no matter your race, religion, ancestry, class, or education, in God's eyes, we are all equal, loved, and valued by our Creator. In fact, our founders said just this in the Declaration of Independence. They wrote:

> We hold these truths to be self-evident, that all men are created equal, that they are endowed by their Creator with certain unalienable Rights, that among these are Life, Liberty and the pursuit of Happiness.--That to secure these rights, Governments are instituted among Men, deriving their just powers from the consent of the governed, --That whenever any Form of Government becomes destructive of these ends, it is the Right

> of the People to alter or to abolish it, and to institute new Government, laying its foundation on such principles and organizing its powers in such form, as to them shall seem most likely to effect their Safety and Happiness.

Need anyone ever say more? The Declaration of Independence and the U.S. Constitution are divinely inspired documents that represent the peak of human thinking. Only the Bible, which is inspired by God, can better capture the greatest hopes for humanity. As humans and Americans, we have been blessed with a just form of government that has done so much good. But at this time, our government is failing. In part, it is failing because we have a politicized judiciary. But what does that mean?

Today, a new philosophy has taken over. Rather than the Constitution, many people find their inspiration in something called intersectionality. Here is one definition:

Intersectionality (or intersectional theory) is a term first coined in 1989 by American civil rights advocate and leading scholar of critical race theory, Kimberlé Williams Crenshaw, who has also been a law professor.

It is the study of overlapping or intersecting social identities and related systems of oppression, domination, or discrimination. The theory suggests that—and seeks to examine how—various biological, social, and cultural categories such as gender, race, class, ability, sexual orientation, religion, caste, age, nationality, and other sectarian axes of identity interact on multiple and often simultaneous levels.

In other words, intersectional theory asserts that people are often disadvantaged by multiple sources of oppression: their race, class, gender identity, sexual orientation, religion, and other identity markers. Intersectionality recognizes that identity markers (e.g., "woman" and "Black") do not exist independently of each other and that each informs the other, often creating a complex convergence of oppression.

Compare that word salad to the elegance of the Declaration of Independence. But the word salad is also enormously consequential. As we see every day on the news, people find new ways to distinguish themselves from others and to divide people along these lines of race, gender, and identity. Intersectionality is a divisive concept that seeks to divide people by defining them as either oppressors or oppressed. But it is also one of the dominant themes of today's Liberals.

Here is an excerpt from the Democrat Party's current platform:

> Democrats are committed to ending discrimination on the basis of race, ethnicity,

national origin, religion, language, gender, age, sexual orientation, gender identity, or disability status. We will appoint U.S. Supreme Court justices and federal judges who look like America, are committed to the rule of law, will uphold individual civil rights and civil liberties as essential components of a free and democratic society, and will respect and enforce foundational precedents, including Brown v. Board of Education and Roe v. Wade.[6]

One commentator described the Democrat Party as being the "more socially and economically liberal of America's two parties and generally favor enforced rights for racial and ethnic minorities, women, LGBTQIA+ people, abortion access, and collective bargaining by workers."[7] This emphasis on, and enforcement of, rights for diverse populations is practically the definition of intersectionality. And as we will explore below, the party in power appoints judges it believes will issue legal decisions favorable to that party's political goals. This applies equally to both parties.

The orientation of the Democrat Party on intersectionality runs counter to traditionally-minded Americans who think about God, family, and country in that order. It also runs counter to the belief of the Founding Fathers that we all have inalienable rights endowed upon us by our Creator. But for a people to be guided by what makes them unique (such as being a wise Latina), as opposed to what they have in common (creation of a just and durable society committed to human flourishing)—division is inevitable.

As you can tell, I am a Conservative. I believe in the Constitution, and I align myself with the philosophy of equality of all people espoused by the founders. My views were formed by my upbringing among poor urban Appalachians in Covington, Kentucky. This urban working-class environment offered its own perspective on decision-making. I know people from working-class families who fought very hard to live a good life.

Ironically, I also know a wise Latina. My wife was born and raised in Puerto Rico. These factors have influenced my life and how I make decisions. But I try exceedingly hard to think more like Alexander Hamilton than like today's liberal thought leaders who focus on a "lived experience."

It is absurd to believe your "lived" life is richer or confers more wisdom than someone else's life. I do not believe a combination of race, gender, and sexual orientation makes any person a better decision-maker. To claim that being a "wise Latina" somehow confers a better perspective on decision-making does not show wisdom; instead, it shows conceit and intellectual immaturity.

Few people would ever guess I was once trapped in a chain-link enclosure and had to escape three teenagers with baseball bats who literally wanted to kill me, because my friends and I managed to win a pickup basketball game. Does that traumatic experience make me a better decision-maker than my friend whose brother was killed in an auto accident, which in turn caused his family to disintegrate?

No. Instead of being formed by our "lived" experiences, we must be formed by principles and the type of truth we learn in the Bible, and from the ancient Greeks and Romans. Those are some of the texts the Founding Fathers relied upon. And that is the problem we confront today. Instead of relying upon the wisdom of the ages, we rely upon our Bronx childhood and whether we are diverse in some way.

My point is—when you think about the "Judge" as a political figure, you must think about what type of politics to which that judge subscribes. Is she informed by her lived experience or by her Christian upbringing? Are her politics informed by classical learning, or are they based upon intersectionality? Federal judges, thanks to Alexander Hamilton and the Founding Fathers, have massive power to shape society. They are solely responsible for deciding on the constitutionality of laws and how the law applies to all of us. The U.S. Supreme Court is a colossus created at the founding of our nation, and ruled by generally brilliant people. Nonetheless, they are mere mortals, and their decisions are shaped by their lived experiences and, of course, their politics.

How is that politics, or philosophy of governance, expressed today? In modern times, the judicial branch struggles under a burden of partisanship, with two societies established to promote political views: the Federalist Society and the American Constitution Society. The former claims to be conservative, while the other is positioned to be more traditionally liberal. Depending on which side of the aisle you lean towards or how involved you are in the happenings of the judicial branch, you may not be aware of either of these two groups.

Let's start by reviewing the Federalist Society, and how they summarize who they are:

> "The Federalist Society holds that law schools and the legal profession are currently strongly dominated by a form of orthodox liberal ideology which advocates a centralized and uniform society. While some members of the academic community have dissented from these views, by and large they are taught simultaneously with (and indeed as if they were) the law."[8]

This is a bold position to take, and as a practicing lawyer, I do not fully agree that the legal profession is *dominated* by people who want a centralized and uniform society.

Indeed, many law professors are bound up by liberal ideology. I am not certain, but this may be a coastal or Washington, D.C. issue. What I can say is that an extremely polarized and politicized set of legislators in the U.S. Senate is responsible for the appointment of federal judges. Republicans, including President Trump, have pulled their judicial nominees largely from the ranks of the Federalist Society.

So, what are the members of this society all about, and what do they believe? They claim the following:

> "… a group of conservatives and libertarians interested in the current state of the legal order. It is founded on the principles that the state exists to preserve freedom, that the separation of governmental powers is central to our Constitution, and that it is emphatically the province and duty of the judiciary to say what the law is, not what it should be. The Society seeks both to promote an awareness of these principles and to further their application through its activities."[9]

The Federalist Society's beliefs seek to track closely with the Constitution and are based upon the same principles that guided our nation's founding.

Conversely, we have another legal organization that influences whom we appoint to the federal bench: the American Constitution Society. Its stated purpose is to be:

> "the nation's foremost progressive legal organization, with a diverse nationwide network that includes nearly 200 student and lawyer chapters, and progressive lawyers, students, judges, scholars, elected officials, and advocates."[10]

This is the mirror image of the Federalist Society, but the American Constitution Society's stated mission and vision are:

> "support and advocate for laws and legal systems that redress the founding failures of our Constitution, strengthen our democratic legitimacy, uphold the rule of law, and realize the promise of equality for all, including people of color, women, LGBTQ+ people, people with disabilities, and other historically excluded communities."[11]

> "...a multi-racial, representative democracy that includes: A judiciary that reflects the diversity of the public it serves, vindicates fundamental freedoms, protects democratic guardrails, upholds the rule of law, and interprets the U.S. Constitution through the lens of history and lived experience; Democratic institutions that advance

equity and justice, uphold the rule of law, and guard against the abuse of power; and a robust and diverse legal civil society that actively promotes progressive legal transformation and redress of the founding failures of our Constitution and of our laws and legal systems."[12]

Did you catch the reference to "lived experience"? That is code for intersectionality. The gist of the American Constitution Society's platform is to elect and appoint judges who will support intersectionality. They see our founding, and its emphasis on the equality of all men, as a failure. The differences between the Federalist Society and the American Constitution Society could not be greater. These two societies compete to appoint judges who will rule in a manner consistent with their stated principles. One is inclusive, and the other is divisive. I think the reader's political persuasion will determine which society is which.

The competition between these two societies absolutely politicizes the court. But does it have a practical effect? The American Constitution Society put out a study that asserted:

"[t]oday's state court elections are more intensely politicized than ever, and rising campaign spending increases pressures on elected judges to promote their parties' interests in state court. It is no surprise then that party favoritism and party

campaign finance plays a major factor in how state
judges decide the growing number of election
disputes litigated in state court."[13]

The study cited campaign finance records that show
contributions to judicial contests have expanded dramatically
in the past 25 years. It also shows that the parties are
competing to win these races. So, politicization does have a
practical effect on the judiciary. It funds state judicial elections
and tries to have the preferred type of judge elected with the
expectation that they will vote consistently with their political
beliefs.

We also see politicization in the appointment of federal
judges, especially those appointed to the Supreme Court. We
have all read about the terrible process those nominated to
the federal bench must endure. This is the result of
politicization. Democrats, more so than Republicans, have
engaged in the politics of personal destruction to keep the
most qualified conservative judges off the bench.

This was seen with the appointment of Justice Clarence
Thomas and the bizarre allegations made against him by
Anita Hill. Similarly, the Democrats in the U.S. Senate
unfairly and brutally attacked Brett Kavanaugh when he was
nominated to the Supreme Court. Like with Justice Thomas,
the Democrats tried to smear now Justice Kavanaugh with
absurd allegations of sexual misconduct.

By contrast, the Republicans have been less caustic with Democrats nominated to the Supreme Court. Justice Kavanaugh was appointed by a slim majority of 50 to 48, with one not voting, and one voting "present." Only one Democrat, Senator Joe Manchin of West Virginia, voted for Justice Kavanaugh. Justice Ketanji Brown Jackson did little better. She also had a slim majority of 53 to 47. Only three Republicans supported her nomination. But there were no manufactured allegations of sexual misconduct or the like levied against her. The point is that the process is politicized, and the voters don't like it. The highly contentious nature of the appointment process sours everyday people and delegitimizes the process, because people do not trust it.

A recent study published in *The Annual Review of Political Science: Bias and Judging*, reached an interesting conclusion that I think is consistent with my views expressed above. Citing the study:

> How do we know whether judges of different backgrounds are biased? We review the substantial political science literature on judicial decision making, paying close attention to how judges' demographics and ideology can influence or structure their decision making. As the research demonstrates, characteristics such as race, ethnicity, and gender can sometimes predict judicial decision making in limited kinds of cases;

however, the literature also suggests that these characteristics are far less important in shaping or predicting outcomes than is ideology (or partisanship), which in turn correlates closely with gender, race, and ethnicity.

This leads us to conclude that assuming judges of different backgrounds are biased because they rule differently is questionable. Given that the application of the law rarely provides one objectively correct answer, it is no surprise that judges' decisions vary according to their personal backgrounds and, more importantly, according to their ideology.[14]

It's pretty eye-opening when a credible study has such blatant things to say about the politicization of the judiciary. What's the practical effect? Let's look once again at Nick Sandmann's case against the mainstream media. After five years of fighting, the Federal Sixth Circuit Court of Appeals issued a decision adverse to Nick. It found that the statements Native American Nathan Phillips made, which were repeated by the media defendants asserting that Nick blocked Phillips and "prevented his retreat," were only Phillips' opinion, and thus not actionable.

This, despite having 14 different camera angles showing Nick did not move one inch. So, how could anyone have the opinion that Nick blocked Phillips? I know; it makes no sense.

But were the judges political or biased? I don't know, but if we consider the findings of the study cited above, they might have been. The judge who wrote the majority opinion was a woman appointed by President Barack Obama. The judge who joined in the opinion against Nick was a Black woman appointed by President Biden. The dissenting judge who favored Nick was a white man appointed by President George W. Bush.

Certainly, these judges are all brilliant and skilled, but are they biased by their "lived experience" or political ideologies? We really will never know. But we do know that, in general, the politicized process of electing and appointing judges has created a judiciary that is influenced by its ideology.

Chapter Notes

1 James Madison Alexander Hamilton, Clinton Rossiter, John Jay, and Charles Kesler, The Federalist Papers (New York: Signet Classics, and imprint of New American Library a division of Penguin Group (USA), 2005).

2 Alexander Hamilton.

3 Spoken casually by Sonia Sotomayor at the annual Mario G. Olmos Law and Cultural Diversity Lecture at UC-Berkeley in 2001

4 In a letter to his friend Benjamin Rush in 1806, Adams exclaimed that "I lose all patience when I think of a bastard brat of a Scotch peddler."

5 2024, "Intellectual Foundations of the American Founding," accessed May 24, 2024, https://constitutioncenter.org/the-constitution/historic-document-library/time-period/intellectual-foundations.

6 "Healing the Soul of America," 2024, accessed May 24, 2024, https://democrats.org/where-we-stand/party-platform/healing-the-soul-of-america/.

7 Peter Weber, "What Do the Democrats Stand For?," last modified Oct 9, 2023, 2023, accessed May 24, 2024, https://theweek.com/politics/what-do-the-democrats-stand-for.

8 Federalist Society, "About Us," Federalist Society, 2024, accessed May 24, 2024, https://fedsoc.org/about-us#Background.

9 "About Acs," American Constitution Society, 2024, accessed May 24, 2024, https://www.acslaw.org/about-us/.

10 , "About Acs."

11 , "About Acs."

12 , "About Acs."

13 Joanna Shepherd, and Michael S. Kang, "Partisan Justice," accessed May 24, 2024, https://www.acslaw.org/analysis/reports/partisan-justice/.

14 Allison P. Harris, and Maya Sen, "Bias and Judging," Annual Review of Political Science 22 (28 May 2019, https://ssrn.com/abstract=3394078.

A HOUSE BUILT ON SAND

THE BASIS OF MODERN DEFAMATION LAW

"Injustice anywhere is a threat to justice everywhere. We are caught in an inescapable network of mutuality, tied in a single garment of destiny. Whatever affects one directly, affects all indirectly."
- Martin Luther King Jr.

Few, if any, periods in American history have witnessed more profound political, technological, and social change than the 1960s. Technological innovation gave us leaps forward in consumer electronics, computing, medicine, and, of course, space travel. It was the decade that gave rise to the ballistic missile submarine and an expanse of nuclear arms fueled by the doctrine of mutually assured destruction. The sound of music changed forever with the British Invasion, Psychedelic Rock, Funk, Surf music, and the rise of new musical instruments.

The country was rocked by frequent political assassinations, as the Vietnam War abroad and

Counterculture protests at home threatened overall social peace. Second-wave feminism gained massive momentum, sexual freedom exploded, and environmental issues gained room in the popular zeitgeist. As is well known, the civil rights movement improved nearly every aspect of American culture (from entertainment to education), with many important spheres of life beginning the process of desegregation.

My father was very involved in the civil rights movement. He volunteered for the American Civil Liberties Union to fight for racial justice. The local paper always referred to him as "Lib-lawyer Steve McMurtry." I have vivid memories from when I was a child of participating in anti-war protests, political organizing meetings, and my parents hosting visiting civil rights leaders. One of my earliest recollections was marching on the Covington IRS building with a sea of protesters. When I saw armed soldiers on the roof of the building, I was scared. Those were serious times, indeed.

It was a decade with so much rapid change that it was difficult to predict where it was all headed, and what the consequences of all the changes would be. In fact, no small amount of analysis has been dedicated to tracing the roots of modern society to the upheaval of that decade.

While many of these changes are known to the general public, an often lesser-emphasized subject is that the early 1960s were also a time of significant judicial activism by the

Supreme Court, which was led by Chief Justice Earl Warren. The Warren Court was known for its progressive rulings on civil rights and liberties, including the landmark decision in *Brown v. Board of Education* (1954), which declared state laws establishing separate public schools for Black and white students to be unconstitutional. In the midst of this tumultuous decade, the High Court's willingness to tackle controversial issues to protect individual rights set the stage to revisit and redefine the standards of defamation law.

The press also played a crucial role in documenting and publicizing the civil rights struggles. Media coverage brought national attention to the brutality faced by African American protesters and the systemic racism prevalent in Southern states. This coverage was instrumental in swaying public opinion in favor of civil rights legislation. However, it also made the press a target for those opposing desegregation and civil rights. Emotions were running high as stagnating ideals were being challenged, and new standards were solidifying a stronger sense of the intrinsic value we all share as human beings.

At the start of the decade, a full-page ad was submitted to *The New York Times* by the Committee to Defend Martin Luther King. At the time, this ad, titled *Heed Their Rising Voices*,[1] was a common format for such appeals, designed to attract maximum attention. The advertisement was created to highlight the escalating civil rights movement and to draw national attention to the plight of African Americans in the South. It also sought to solicit support for the movement.

Th ad detailed the violent repression of civil rights protests, highlighting incidents such as the arrest of Dr. King on perjury charges,[2] which was widely viewed as a tactic to undermine his leadership and intimidate the movement. It included emotional appeals and called on the public to financially and morally support the cause. Its endorsements from prominent figures across various fields lent it significant credibility. The 100 or so signers included some of the most popular figures of the time: Harry Belafonte, Marlon Brando, Nat King Cole, Sammy Davis Jr., Dr. Harry Emerson Fosdick, Eartha Kitt, Sidney Poitier, Jackie Robinson, and even Mrs. Eleanor Roosevelt.

The hope was to galvanize public opinion and financial backing from a broad audience, emphasizing both the urgency and the moral imperative of the movement.

As it was a common practice, *The Times* had established procedures for vetting such advertisements, but in this case, the fact-checking process was not as rigorous as usual.[3] This oversight led to the inclusion of some factual inaccuracies in the ad, such as minor errors about events and the involvement of certain individuals. Despite these inaccuracies, the ad was approved and published on March 29, 1960. The decision to run the ad was influenced by *The Times*' editorial stance, which was generally supportive of the civil rights movement and critical of segregationist policies.

L.B. Sullivan, the Public Affairs Commissioner of Montgomery, who supervised the police department, felt that the ad defamed him, even though he was not explicitly named. He sued *The New York Times* and four African American ministers whose names appeared in the advertisement,[4] claiming the inaccuracies harmed his reputation. An Alabama jury awarded Sullivan $500,000 in damages, a decision upheld by the Alabama Supreme Court.[5]

As it turns out, this behavior was also pretty common practice. In response to the growing civil rights activism, many Southern politicians and public officials engaged in a campaign of "massive resistance" to desegregation. This included using legal and extralegal measures to maintain the status quo of racial segregation, and silence dissent. The libel suits against *The New York Times*, and other media outlets were part of this broader strategy to intimidate and silence critics of segregation.

Libel suits were an abusive but effective tool to silence critics, media coverage of segregation, and civil rights abuses. This strategy aimed to curb the influence of the Northern press and prevent the spread of pro-civil rights narratives. This meant that the ability for journalists to report on important topics, like civil rights abuses, was under constant threat of crippling lawsuits from private citizens and public officials.

The U.S. Supreme Court agreed to hear the case, and in a unanimous decision delivered by Justice William Brennan on March 9, 1964, the Court reversed the Alabama court's ruling. The *New York Times Co. v. Sullivan* decision is widely regarded as one of the most important Supreme Court rulings of the 20th century. It significantly reshaped American libel law by establishing the "actual malice" standard, which requires public officials to prove that a defamatory statement was made with knowledge of its falsity or reckless disregard for the truth. It was no longer whether or not the statement was true or false (something relatively easy to prove), but instead focused on what the *intent* was of publishing the inaccurate information.

This was a drastic departure from the common law standard, which did not require proof of intent or recklessness. This new standard was a significantly harder thing to demonstrate and has had enduring implications for modern defamation law. While the goal was a good one— freedom of the press in service to lofty ideals—the practical implications have created a difficult and tenuous balance between protecting individual reputations, safeguarding free speech, and press freedoms. The decision reinforced the role of the press as a watchdog and a critical player in the democratic process.

The decision also underscored the importance of protecting free speech and free press, especially in the context of public debate about government and public officials. The Court emphasized that debate should be "uninhibited, robust, and wide-open,"[6] even if it includes vehement, caustic, and sometimes unpleasantly sharp attacks on public officials. Again, this is an excellent idea in theory and a lofty goal, but without equivalent changes in the law to protect private citizens, the press could declare open season on nearly any American citizen, with only their journalistic integrity to keep them in check. Maybe that worked for the '60s, but any such integrity now seems like mythology of a distant past.

Fast Forward to the Modern Era

The "actual malice" standard set by *New York Times Co. v. Sullivan* has become the cornerstone of defamation law in the United States, influencing numerous subsequent cases and legal interpretations. The principles established in *Sullivan* have also been extended to *all* public figures, not just public officials. This has made it extremely difficult for public figures to win defamation lawsuits. We have robust protections for the press and foster a more open and critical public discourse.

But, sixty years later, the way information flows has changed dramatically. Nearly any person on the planet can call themselves a journalist, have global reach through the Internet, and find themselves in the near-global public eye (whether they want it or not). Section 230 of the Communications Decency Act, created in the infancy of the Internet, grants immunity for content hosted on web platforms that are also enjoyed by large-scale media. Again, on its face, this sounds like a laudable approach to maintaining free speech in a complex system of society.

We have entered an era as vitriolic and divided as the 1960s, and the same journalistic integrity on which *Sullivan* was assumed is no longer in place. The stage is set to ensure that everyone wins, with the exception of the everyday American citizen, who is just trying to make it through life without getting canceled, defamed, and financially destroyed.

Supporters of *Sullivan*, like Justice Sonia Sotomayor, defend the decision and argue that it remains crucial for protecting free speech, especially in an era when the press continues to play a vital role in holding power to account. In a recent concurrence, she reaffirmed the importance of the actual malice standard for protecting free speech and press freedoms.[7] Sotomayor's position underscores the significance of *Sullivan* in maintaining robust public debate and preventing the chilling effect that easier defamation claims could have on the media. But in recent years, the ruling has faced growing criticism. Some conservative jurists, notably Justices Clarence Thomas and Neil Gorsuch, have called for the decision to be revisited.

Justice Thomas has argued that the actual malice standard departs from the original understanding of the First Amendment, and has rendered libel law ineffective in deterring falsehoods. He has repeatedly called for the Supreme Court to reconsider the ruling, arguing that it lacks a constitutional foundation and was a policy-driven decision masquerading as constitutional law. Thomas believes that the decision and its extensions were not grounded in the original understanding of the First Amendment. He has expressed these views in multiple opinions, including a 2019 concurring opinion and a 2023 dissent, where he criticized the Court's reliance on *Sullivan* in unrelated cases. He contends that states should have more leeway to balance robust public discourse with protecting reputations. It could be argued that this is even more relevant in today's media landscape, which is characterized by the rapid spread of misinformation and the decline of traditional news outlets.[8]

Justice Neil Gorsuch has also questioned the relevance of the *Sullivan* decision in the modern media landscape. He has argued that the media environment has changed significantly since 1964, with the rise of social media and 24-hour news cycle, which has led to the proliferation of falsehoods. Gorsuch has suggested that the actual malice standard established by *Sullivan* might be outdated and that the Court should revisit the decision to address these changes. He suggests that the current standards may no longer be suitable for today's environment, where anyone can become a "public figure" by gaining notoriety online. This evolution raises questions about whether the protections established in *Sullivan* still serve their intended purpose.[9]

As the law has evolved from *Sullivan*, public officials and public figures are not only governed by the standard, but so are people "who thrust themselves into the vortex" of a public controversy. In my cases, opponents have argued that responding to a Facebook post is the same as thrusting yourself into the vortex. The point is that many private people can find themselves exposed to the actual malice standard without even realizing they are turning themselves into limited-purpose public figures. These real-world examples go to Justice Gorsuch's point that the current standards may no longer serve their intended purpose.

A recent critique of *Sullivan* authored by legal historian, Samantha Barbas, titled *Actual Malice: Civil Rights and Freedom of the Press in New York Times v. Sullivan*, highlighted some of the key criticisms leveled against *Sullivan*:

- It changed the common law principles that were in effect and replaced them with a standard crafted by the lawyers for *The New York Times*.

- "An area of the law that had been left up to the states was nationalized, . ."

- It permanently changed the value of an individual's reputation from highly prized to being subjected to lowered standards, especially for public figures.

- It freed the media from having to do the hard work of digging for the truth.

Despite the criticisms from Justices Thomas and Gorsuch, the Supreme Court has consistently declined to revisit the *Sullivan* decision. In recent cases, the Court has reaffirmed the principles established by *Sullivan*, indicating that a majority of the justices still support the decision's core tenets. This hesitation is understandable. Any move to overturn or modify the *Sullivan* standard would have significant implications for free speech and press freedoms in the United States. As Americans, we value the free press, and freedom of speech even more. We will face more civil rights issues in the future, and we will need free discussion (public and private) to make our way through.

But I believe revisiting this landmark decision is inevitable. As misinformation becomes more prevalent, the conversation around modifying the standards set by this case is likely to continue, reflecting ongoing concerns about the balance between free speech and accountability in the digital age. Ironically, the rulings' potential to shield false and damaging statements from legal consequences is effectively creating a modern civil rights issue of its own.

Citizens are not safe to express their views, or even be a young man wearing a hat in public, without having their lives destroyed. Misinformation and knee-jerk reactions by corporations to protect their bottom line have led to financial and reputational harm for those who even merely *appear* to have views considered unacceptable by whatever mob mentality rules the day.

New York Times Co. v. Sullivan is a constant subject of extensive legal and academic analysis, with scholars examining its implications from every angle, including free speech, press freedom, reputational harms, and democratic governance. The case is frequently discussed in law schools and constitutional law courses as a pivotal example of judicial protection of civil liberties. But I believe it is time for the American public to become more familiar with it, understand its history, and begin to call attention to the reforms that need to take place to balance freedom of speech with the right to protect our reputations. Anything less is simply un-American.

Chapter Notes

1 Full text available at: https://www.archives.gov/exhibits/documented-rights/ exhibit/section4/detail/heed-rising-voices-transcript.html

2 "State of Alabama V. M. L. King, Jr., Nos. 7399 and 9593," Stanford University (The Martin Luther King, Jr. Research and Education Institute), accessed May 24, 2024, https://kinginstitute.stanford.edu/state-alabama-v-m-l-king-jr-nos-7399-and-9593.

3 "New York Times V. Sullivan (1964)," Jack Miller Center, accessed May 24, 2024, https://jackmillercenter.org/cd-resources/new-york-times-v-sullivan-1964/.

4 Daniel Aharonoff, "The Landmark Case That Redefined Free Speech: Analyzing Nyt V. Sullivan," last modified Jan 3, 2024, 2024, accessed May 24, 2024, https://www.aharonofftechtales.com/2024/01/the-landmark-case-that-redefined-free.html.

5 New York Times Co. v. Sullivan, 376 U.S. 254 (1964)

6 New York Times.

7 Counterman v. Colorado, 600 U.S. ___ (2023)

8 Berisha v. Lawson, 141 S. Ct. 2424, 2424-25, 2425-30 (2021) (Thomas, J., dissenting) (Gorsuch, J., dissenting); Two Justices Say Supreme Court Should Reconsider Landmark Decision, N.Y. Times, Jul. 2, 2021; see also McKee v. Cosby, 139 S. Ct. 675, 676 (2019) (Thomas, J., concurring).

9 Berisha.

ASLEEP AT THE WHEEL

OLD LAWS AND MOB RULE

"People will generally accept facts as truth only if the facts agree with what they already believe."
- Andy Rooney

There's an old cartoon produced by Walt Disney in 1958 that celebrates the folklore of Paul Bunyan and his Great Ox, Babe.[1] For those who haven't seen it, the cartoon is a brilliant throwback to a time of hand-drawn animation, beautiful orchestral scores, and witty writing that rhymed so seamlessly you barely noticed it.

In this particular cartoon, the legend of the giant, Paul Bunyan, beautifully weaves tall tales of how the giant and his big blue ox helped shape the North American Landscape, and eventually how his expertise as a lumberjack simultaneously helped provide lumber for growing western towns while clearing enough timber to provide ample farmlands for a growing American populace.

The cartoon is full of the type of whimsy you'd expect to hear from your grandpa while sitting by a campfire as he puffed on a pipe and you roasted one too many marshmallows. The story takes a sad turn toward the end, however, when steam technology finally catches up with poor Paul Bunyan. In a thrilling competition between an ordinary city dweller wielding what can only be described as a steam-powered predecessor of the modern-day chainsaw and the gigantic, one-of-a-kind Paul Bunyan, the city dweller narrowly defeats Paul. Technology not only reigns supreme in the cartoon, but the implication is clear—with technology, literally anyone can be superhuman.

Watching that cartoon all these years later, I can't help but draw different parallels in the year 2024 as I sit surrounded by technology that rivals (sometimes surpasses) some episodes of Star Trek. I don't think it's hyperbole to say that the explosion of the Internet has quite literally redefined how almost everyone in America lives their lives.

At the end of the last century, Congress enacted the Communications Decency Act of 1996. A prominent piece of that act was Section 230. In essence, Section 230 protects internet platforms from liability for many things third parties say or do on them. One of the main points I made in an earlier chapter is that while many large corporations (specifically social media companies) spend time protecting themselves as well as playing political games of fact-checking and ideological censorship, individual citizens suffer from deplatforming and being silenced. However, there is another, equally chilling side to the way this law is both structured and being interpreted.

Step Aside, Old Man

Twenty-eight years. That's how long it's been since Section 230 was first penned. At the time, there were approximately 45 million internet users worldwide. To put things in perspective, by the year 2000 that user base had grown to roughly 407 million users and was present in 218 of 246 countries across the globe (more than half of that user base was in the United States).[2] And, since we're having fun with numbers, *Forbes* estimates that there will be 5.35 billion internet users in 2024.[3]

It wasn't until 1994 that the White House of the United States launched its first website. If we stop and think how different things were just twenty-eight years ago, things get strange. For video rentals, Blockbuster Video reigned supreme (there's now one Blockbuster still in operation, located in Bend, Oregon—and it survives due to a strong dose of nostalgia and goodwill from the community). 1-800-COLLECT was a thriving business, and compact discs (CDs) were the main way to hear the latest hit from your favorite band. The term "viral" only referred to sickness, and the closest thing to wireless communication was the pager. Terms like social media, blog, vlog, and podcasts would have been terms better suited for a wildly speculative work of fiction.

I genuinely don't think Chris Cox and Ron Wyden (the framers of Section 230) could have foreseen what the Internet has become. I previously discussed how laws regarding social media are outdated (or, more accurately, that there aren't really any correct categories for social media in our laws), specifically for how corporations are likely to misuse them. There is also an incredible gap when it comes to how the rights of individual users are handled.

While it's true that users run the risk of being deplatformed due to the political ideologies of those who run the technologies, the other side of the coin is how opinion, anonymity, and celebrity play into this dynamic. Due to the ease with which virtually any user with access to the Internet can post information, the hope for any sort of safe haven for private citizens has, in essence, been nullified. Content can get posted, do its damage, and fade into the raging river of the Internet within the blink of an eye. But even if the content floats quickly away, the damage caused to ordinary people (often teenagers just wading into the waters of the Internet) is very real.

Here are just a few notable incidents from the last fifteen years:

> Megan Meier: A 13-year-old girl from Missouri who took her own life after being cyberbullied on MySpace by an adult neighbor posing as a teenage boy. The neighbor, along with her daughter, created a fake profile to befriend and later tormented Megan, leading to her suicide in 2006.[4]

> Tyler Clementi: An 18-year-old student at Rutgers University who jumped off the George Washington Bridge in 2010. His roommate had secretly streamed a video of Tyler having a romantic encounter with another man, which was shared online. The public exposure and subsequent bullying contributed to his decision to end his life.[5]

> Audrie Pott: A 15-year-old from California who was sexually assaulted by classmates at a party. Photos of the assault were circulated online, leading to widespread bullying. She hanged herself eight days after the incident in 2012.[6]

> Rehtaeh Parsons: A 17-year-old from Nova Scotia, Canada, who was allegedly raped by four boys who then shared photographs of the assault online. After enduring two years of cyberbullying and a lack of legal action against the perpetrators,

she attempted suicide and died in the hospital in 2013.[7]

Amanda Todd: A 15-year-old from British Columbia, Canada, Amanda posted a video on YouTube detailing her experiences with cyberbullying and sextortion after an individual had blackmailed her with a photo of her breasts. She received further harassment and eventually took her own life in 2012.[8]

I wish I could say the above list is comprehensive. But we all know that is not true. The amount of cyberbullying that happens on a daily basis in high schools across the country could easily be labeled as a national health crisis. But cyberbullying doesn't stop in high school.

In April of 2021, a Columbus, OH, police officer was called to an incident involving two teenage girls. When the officer arrived at the scene, he witnessed two girls embroiled in a fight. As he approached the scene and tried to diffuse the situation, one of the girls, 16-year-old Ma'Khia Bryant, pulled a knife and lunged at the other girl. The officer had no choice but to open fire in order to stop Ms. Bryant from committing a heinous act.

It was a situation every police officer hopes never happens to them. However, in the social justice fervor that was swirling through our nation at the time, many on social media picked up on a story of "white cop shoots teenage black girl."

The frenzy had begun. However, there was one reaction which was particularly appalling. Prominent basketball star Lebron James (with upwards of 50 million followers) tweeted a picture of the police officer, taken as he attempted to bring calm back to the horrendous scene, with the caption, "YOU'RE NEXT #ACCOUNTABILITY." The responsibility of that tweet cannot be overstated. In his desire to flex his social justice muscles, James set the sights of his vast following against a police officer who had just saved a young woman from a violent attack.

I'm pleased to say the response to James' tweet was largely negative. Other prominent figures called attention to just how negligent and ignorant his response was. However, rather than accept responsibility for moving too soon, he took the tweet down and posted what can only be called an excuse (not an apology) for his behavior:

> "ANGER does any of us any good and that includes myself!" James tweeted. "Gathering all the facts and educating does though! My anger still is here for what happened that lil girl. My sympathy for her family and may justice prevail!"[9]

> "I'm so damn tired of seeing Black people killed by
> police. I took the tweet down because its being
> used to create more hate -This isn't about one
> officer. it's about the entire system and they always
> use our words to create more racism. I am so
> desperate for more ACCOUNTABILITY."[10]

I guess, for Mr. James, accountability only flows one way. The litany of offenses perpetrated against private citizens could go on forever.

There is a dream I think almost every person has had at one point or another. You're back in high school, and as you walk down the halls, you suddenly realize you're naked. And just as you realize your lack of clothes, so do the rest of your classmates. I'm sure every one of us who has dreamed that dream has been overwhelmed by gratitude upon waking up and realizing it was all a cruel fiction played by our subconscious.

But in today's world, where there is no accountability and virtually anything you've ever shared can enter the public domain at any time, that dream is a terrifying reality for all too many trusting young people who naively share intimate photos, information and thoughts with people they thought they could trust.

You see, defamation and the Internet are intrinsically linked these days. We have to realize and rectify that these laws are grossly outdated. The first step? Our judges (many of them did not grow up or even start their careers in the digital age) must take responsibility for educating themselves on just how complex the digital space has become.

Just last year, while debating a slew of social media cases, Justice Elena Kagan expressed awareness of the complexities involved in ruling on social media cases, acknowledging the significant role of social media in modern public discourse and the challenges it presents to traditional legal frameworks. During oral arguments, she highlighted the importance of understanding the impact of social media on politics and communication, indicating that the Supreme Court is keenly aware of the need to carefully consider the implications of their decisions in this rapidly evolving digital landscape.

Kagan's comments reflect a broader judicial recognition of the difficulties posed by social media-related cases, especially those involving free speech and the regulation of online platforms. She and other justices have shown an understanding that decisions in these cases could have far-reaching effects on the digital public sphere, underscoring the need for a nuanced approach that balances free speech rights with the realities of modern communication technologies.[11]

The ability of elderly judges and Supreme Court justices to render rulings on modern social media trends depends on various factors:

Legal Principles: Judges and justices base their rulings on legal principles rather than personal familiarity with social media platforms. Their understanding of constitutional rights, legal precedent, and statutory interpretation allows them to analyze cases involving social media through a legal lens.

Legal Briefs and Arguments: Attorneys arguing cases involving social media trends provide comprehensive legal briefs and arguments. These documents outline the relevant facts, legal issues, and precedents, enabling judges to make informed decisions regardless of their personal familiarity with social media.

Judicial Research and Assistance: Judges and justices have access to law clerks and legal research resources. They can rely on their clerks to research social media trends, technology, and relevant case law to aid in their decision-making process.

Public Discourse and Expert Testimony: Judges may consider public discourse, expert testimony, and amicus curiae briefs when deliberating cases involving social media. These sources provide valuable insights into the societal impact and legal implications of social media trends.

Adaptability and Continual Learning: While judges may not be digital natives, many are adaptable and committed to continual learning. They attend judicial education programs, conferences, and seminars to stay abreast of technological advancements and their legal implications.

Precedent and Legal Framework: Judges rely on precedent and established legal frameworks to guide their decisions. While social media may present novel issues, the underlying legal principles remain consistent, allowing judges to apply existing legal doctrines to new contexts.

Overall, the judiciary's role is to interpret the law impartially and apply it to the facts of each case, regardless of the subject matter's novelty or complexity. While individual judges may not be intimately familiar with modern social media trends, they possess the analytical skills and legal expertise necessary to render informed decisions on such matters.

In the last ten years, there have not been significant Supreme Court rulings that fundamentally alter the principles established by *New York Times v. Sullivan* regarding defamation, particularly in the context of social media and print. The *New York Times v. Sullivan* decision, which requires public figures to prove "actual malice" to succeed in a defamation lawsuit, remains the cornerstone of defamation law in the United States.

However, there have been discussions and dissenting opinions within the Supreme Court about potentially revisiting this standard. Justice Clarence Thomas, in particular, has repeatedly expressed his view that the Court should reconsider the "actual malice" standard established by *New York Times v. Sullivan*. For example, in recent cases like *Berisha v. Lawson* and *McKee v. Cosby*, Thomas has written dissenting opinions arguing that *The New York Times* standard should be reevaluated because it deviates from the historical understanding of defamation law and the original intentions of the First and Fourteenth Amendments.

Digital Vigilantes

I applaud Justice Thomas for his desire to have the Supreme Court take a closer look at some of the landmark cases regarding defamation and how Section 230 is being applied to our current evolution of the digital space. But as I look around, it feels as if our leaders in this area are being more reactive than proactive.

It's a familiar statement—*Nature abhors a vacuum*. In this case, absent any solid legislation or application of existing law, the citizenry will step in to govern themselves. Under normal circumstances, this idea is unsettling. Regarding the digital world, the idea of Mob Rule is downright terrifying. When a lack of legal guidance leads to anonymous individuals banding together to seek swift retribution without fear of accountability, our academic analysis of legal precedent falls apart. This isn't simply a hypothetical situation. Below are just a few more examples of how digital vigilantism has wreaked havoc on real people.

Natasha Tynes

Natasha Tynes, a Jordanian-American author and communications officer, faced severe backlash after a tweet she posted on May 10, 2019. In the tweet, Tynes criticized a Black D.C. Metro employee for eating on the train, a violation of transit rules. She included a photo of the employee, which led to accusations of racism and entitlement.[12]

The incident quickly escalated, with Tynes receiving widespread condemnation on social media. Critics labeled her actions as racist and harmful, particularly towards a Black woman, contributing to the policing of Black bodies. The backlash was intense and swift, with Tynes described as having jeopardized the employee's safety and livelihood.

As a result of the controversy, Tynes' publisher, Rare Bird Books, canceled the distribution of her upcoming novel *They*

Called Me Wyatt, and issued a statement condemning her actions.[13] The union representing Metro workers highlighted that employees often have limited time to eat between shifts, which was not considered in Tynes' complaint.[14]

Tynes later sued her publisher for $13 million, claiming breach of contract and defamation. She stated that the tweet had led to severe personal repercussions, including death threats and being forced to temporarily leave the country.[15] She also expressed regret over the tweet, acknowledging it as poor judgment and apologizing publicly.[16]

While it is widely accepted that the initial post from Ms. Tynes was a mistake (if her beef was with D.C. Metro, focusing her ire on the worker was not a good move), the vitriol she experienced in the ensuing weeks seems like quite the overkill. And to have four years of her life's work erased over one post—a post for which she apologized—lacks any modicum of balance. And I would be remiss to note that Matt Walsh's video, where he urged people never to apologize because the mob will not be satiated, feels quite germane when considering what happened to Ms. Tynes.

John Gibson

John Gibson, the president of Tripwire Interactive, a video game development company known for titles like *Killing*

Floor and *Maneater*, faced significant backlash after he tweeted his support for a controversial Texas abortion law on September 4, 2021. In his tweet, Gibson praised the U.S. Supreme Court's decision not to block a Texas law that bans abortions after six weeks of pregnancy, a time period before many individuals are aware they are pregnant. He identified himself as a "pro-life game developer," which sparked a wave of criticism from both the public and other industry professionals.

The reaction was swift and severe. Shipwright Studios, a collaborator with Tripwire, announced the cancellation of all of its contracts with Tripwire, citing the inability to continue working under the current leadership due to the controversial nature of Gibson's public statements.[17] Torn Banner Studios, another developer associated with Tripwire, also distanced itself from Gibson's views, emphasizing its disagreement and commitment to women's rights.[18]

The backlash led to Gibson stepping down from his role as CEO of Tripwire Interactive just 53 hours after his initial tweet. The company announced his departure, stating that his opinions did not reflect those of Tripwire Interactive and that his comments had disregarded the values of its team, partners, and the broader community. Alan Wilson was appointed as the interim CEO following Gibson's exit.[19]

In this case study, we see the impact mob rule can have, not just on individuals, but on entire corporations. When we see corporations, with leagues of legal counsel, scared of the backlash from a mob seeking nothing but a sacrifice, we begin to understand the power being abused by those filling the legal vacuum.

I'm also reminded of Colleen Oefelein, a literary agent who was fired from her job simply because her managers found out that she had joined Parler and Truth Social[20]—two conservative-leaning social media platforms. In her case, the mob had not even caught wind of the affiliation—but her employers were so afraid of the potential backlash that they released Ms. Oefelein.

Nathan Silvester

Nathan Silvester, a former deputy marshal from Bellevue, Idaho, became the center of significant controversy due to a TikTok video he posted, mocking NBA star LeBron James' comments on a police shooting incident. In the video, Silvester pretended to ask LeBron James for advice on policing, which quickly went viral and drew widespread attention.[21]

The Bellevue Marshal's Office publicly reprimanded Silvester, stating that his actions in the video did not represent the values of their office. They emphasized that they expected their deputies to engage with the public in a friendly and professional manner, which they felt Silvester did not uphold in his video.[22] Following the incident, Silvester was suspended without pay, and a GoFundMe page was set up to support him during his suspension, raising a significant amount of money.[23]

Despite the initial suspension, the situation escalated, and Silvester was eventually fired from the Bellevue Marshal's Office. The official reason given for his termination was for violating city and state policies, although specific details of these violations were not disclosed by the sources.[24] Silvester claimed that he was a victim of cancel culture, suggesting that his dismissal was influenced by the public and media backlash to his video.

I'm not familiar enough with this case to know what the Bellevue Police Department's actual policy says regarding how employees should or should not conduct themselves on social media. However, I believe we will start seeing more and more employers begin to regulate the behavior of their employees as time goes on. Why wouldn't they? Either their employees toe the line and stay "proper," or when they step out of line, it will be an easy termination. Either way, the mob will focus more on the employee than the company.

Gina Carano

Gina Carano, an actress known for her role as Cara Dune in the Disney+ series *The Mandalorian*, was fired from the show by Lucasfilm following a series of controversial social media posts. The controversy primarily stemmed from a post she shared on Instagram, where she compared the current political climate in the U.S. to the persecution of Jews in Nazi Germany.

In her post, she suggested that the way Jews were treated by their neighbors before the Holocaust was akin to how people with certain political views are treated today. This comparison was widely criticized as offensive and inappropriate, leading to a public outcry and the trending hashtag #FireGinaCarano.[25]

Lucasfilm responded by stating that Carano's social media posts, which were being framed as denigrating toward people based on their cultural and religious identities, were abhorrent and unacceptable. Consequently, they announced that she was no longer employed by Lucasfilm and that there were no plans for her to be involved in future projects. Additionally, her agency, UTA, dropped her as a client.[26]

This incident was not Carano's first encounter with social media controversy. Prior to this, she had faced backlash for mocking mask-wearing during the COVID-19 pandemic and for what some called electoral fraud conspiracy theories. She also sparked criticism for mocking the use of preferred pronouns, which she later clarified was not intended to mock trans people, after a conversation with co-star Pedro Pascal.[27]

The case of Ms. Carano has many facets. It's no secret that Disney Corp. has taken a sharp turn to the Left in its governing politics. So, when Ms. Carano's posts went viral, it wasn't only expedient for Disney to part ways with her; it was in line with its ethos. Another aspect to consider is how Ms. Carano's posts were labeled as "antisemitic" when there was absolutely nothing bigoted or antisemitic about them.

To compare the mistreatment of one group with that of another is tone-deaf (after all, we are not so far gone as a nation that people with the "wrong" political beliefs are being put to death), but certainly does not disparage Jewish people. There's a special level of hypocrisy in the way Disney dealt with Carano, when one evaluates the downright disrespect and mockery with which Pedro Pascal attacks those with whom he disagrees via social media. But, since Mr. Pascal's ethics align with Disney's, not a single corrective word is spoken.

If we think back to the beginning of this chapter, I can't help but remember the story of Paul Bunyan. His loss to the steam-powered saw can undoubtedly be seen as a sad narrative regarding how growing technology tends to leave some of our founding principles behind. But there's something else in the story that stands out to me.

After the big competition, as a defeated Paul Bunyan walks off into the distance, we can see the clear-cut forest that was left by the steam-powered saw. It's a dark foreshadowing of how humanity, in our push to continue progressing technology forward, often fails to consider the long-term implications of our actions.

As I look at the digital landscape and the way accountability is being abdicated to mob rule, I can't help but consider what the future may hold if our legislative and judicial leadership does not stand up and begin to take real action. They had their chance with Nick Sandmann, and they didn't take it. I can only hope that the next time an opportunity presents itself, they will act with more urgency.

Chapter Notes

1 Paul Bunyan, (Walt Disney, 1958).

2 "Imagining the Internet's Quick Look at the Early History of the Internet," Elon University, accessed May 2024, 2024, https://www.elon.edu/u/imagining/time-capsule/early-90s/internet-history/.

3 Lexie Pelchen, "Internet Usage Statistics in 2024," last modified Mar 1, 2024, 2024, accessed May 24, 2024, https://www.forbes.com/home-improvement/internet/internet-statistics/.

4 Kirsten Hallmark, "Death by Words: Do United States Statutes Hold Cyberbullies Liable for Their Victims' Suicide?," Houston Law Review, 2023, accessed May 24, 2024, https://houstonlawreview.org/article/73672-death-by-words-do-united-states-statutes-hold-cyberbullies-liable-for-their-victims-suicide.

5 Ariel Schonfeld et al., "Cyberbullying and Adolescent Suicide," Journal of the American Academy of Psychiatry and the Law Online (2023), https://dx.doi.org/10.29158/jaapl.220078-22.

6 "Audrie Pott Suicide: Three Teens Arrested for Alleged Sexual Assault of Calif. Girl Who Committed Suicide," last modified Apr 12, 2013, 2013, accessed May 24, 2024, https://www.cbsnews.com/news/audrie-pott-suicide-three-teens-arrested-for-alleged-sexual-assault-of-calif-girl-who-committed-suicide/.

7 Elizabeth Chiu, "The Legacy of Rehtaeh Parsons," CBC News, 2018, accessed May 24, 2024, https://newsinteractives.cbc.ca/longform/five-years-gone/.

8 Hallmark

9 LeBron James (@KingJames), "Anger Does Any of Us ...," X (Twitter), Apr 21, 2021, 2021, https://x.com/KingJames/status/1385011051087810561.

10 LeBron James (@KingJames), "I'm So Damn Tired ...," X (Twitter), Apr 21, 2021, 2021, https://x.com/KingJames/status/1385013333007343619.

11 O'Connor-Ratcliff v. Garnier, 601 U.S. ___ (2024); Lindke v. Freed 2023 (Oral Arguments)

12 "Us Author Loses Book Deal for Tweet-Shaming," last modified May 13, 2019, 2019, accessed May 24, 2024, https://www.bbc.com/news/world-us-canada-48257825.

13 Tod Perry, "Writer's Career in Jeopardy after Tweeting About a Black Metro Worker Eating on the Train.," last modified May 20, 2019, 2019, accessed May 24, 2024, https://www.upworthy.com/writer-s-career-in-jeopardy-after-tweeting-about-a-black-metro-worker-eating-on-the-train.

14 Tasneem Nashrulla, "The Writer Who Lost Her Book Deal after Calling out a Dc Metro Worker for Eating on the Train Is Suing the Publisher for $13 Million," last modified Jun 9, 2019, 2019, accessed May 24, 2024, https://www.buzzfeednews.com/article/tasneemnashrulla/dc-metro-writer-tweet-eating-train-book-sue-publisher.

15 Nashrulla

16 Nashrulla

17 James Batchelor, "Shipwright Studios Cuts Ties with Tripwire Interactive over President's Anti-Abortion Views," last modified Sep 6, 2021, 2021, accessed May 24, 2024, https://www.gamesindustry.biz/shipwright-studios-cuts-ties-with-tripwire-interactive-over-presidents-anti-abortion-views.

18 Khristopher J. Brooks, "Tripwire Interactive Ceo Steps down after Supporting Texas Abortion Law," last modified Sep 7, 2021, 2021, accessed May 24, 2024, https://www.cbsnews.com/news/tripwire-texas-abortion-john-gibson-gaming-tweet/.

19 Alisha Rahaman Sarkar, "Tech Ceo and Self-Proclaimed 'Pro-Life Gamer' Steps down after Backing Texas Abortion Law," Independent, last modified Tuesday 07 September 2021, 2021, accessed May 24, 2024, https://www.independent.co.uk/news/world/americas/tripwire-ceo-texas-abortion-law-b1915476.html.

20 "Literary Agent Fired for Joining Parler Tells Her Story," New Tolerance Campaign, May 242024, https://newtolerance.org/literary-agent-fired-for-joining-parler-tells-her-story/.

21 Jordan Boyd, "Idaho Cop Suspended for Viral Tiktok Mocking Lebron James' Police Threat," last modified Apr 29, 2021, 2021, accessed May 24, 2024, https://thefederalist.com/2021/04/29/idaho-cop-suspended-for-viral-tiktok-mocking-lebron-james-police-threat/.

22 Jacob Scholl, "That Idaho Police Officer's Video About Lebron James? His Employer Isn't Happy About It," last modified Apr 29, 2021, 2021, accessed May 24, 2024, https://www.idahostatesman.com/news/northwest/idaho/article251037234.html.

23 Scholl

24 Cammy Pedroja, "Nate Silvester, Cop Who Mocked Lebron James, Fired for Violating City and State Policies," Lipstick Alley, 2021, accessed May 24, 2024, https://www.lipstickalley.com/threads/nate-silvester-cop-who-mocked-lebron-james-fired-for-violating-city-and-state-policies.4558658/.

25 Lee Brown, "See Gina Carano's Tweets and Posts That Got Her Fired from 'the Mandalorian'," last modified Feb 11, 2021, 2021, accessed May 24, 2024, https://nypost.com/2021/02/11/see-gina-caranos-tweets-and-posts-that-got-her-fired/.

26 Daniel Holloway, "Lucasfilm, Uta Drop 'Mandalorian' Star Gina Carano Following Offensive Social Media Posts," last modified Feb 10, 2021, 2021, accessed May 24, 2024, https://variety.com/2021/tv/news/mandalorian-gina-carano-1234905589/.

27 Toby Moses, "Gina Carano Fired from the Mandalorian after 'Abhorrent' Social Media Posts," last modified Feb 11, 2021, 2021, accessed May 24, 2024, https://www.theguardian.com/tv-and-radio/2021/feb/11/gina-carano-fired-from-the-mandalorian-after-abhorrent-social-media-posts.

UNSETTLED ISSUES

WANDERING THE WASTELAND
WITHOUT LANDMARKS

*"A Bill of Rights that means what the majority
wants it to mean is worthless."*
- Antonin Scalia

There is a local coffee shop that has a strange parking lot configuration. Along the front of the shop, there are clearly delineated lines for about fifteen vehicles. Due to the shop's popularity, the lot often fills well beyond those fifteen spots. Luckily, the lot is quite wide—so much so that dedicated patrons are able to parallel park on the other side of the lot, which adds about four more spaces (sometimes only three if the cars are spaced far enough apart). Recently, however, there's been a change to this dynamic.

A blue Ford Ranger has begun to park nose-to-curb opposite the main spaces. And when that happens, any other vehicle that chooses to park in the overflow area follows suit.

The result? Instead of allowing only four extra vehicles to park, about ten additional vehicles can fit. At first, this dynamic only occurred when the Ranger would park there. But now, even when the Ranger isn't there, vehicles will pull in nose-to-curb at least half of the time.

The decision of one single patron is beginning to redefine how others use the parking lot, even when that person isn't at the coffee shop. A new and fascinating precedent is being set in the lot. *What's the big deal*, you may ask? Well, given that there isn't any other parking in the area, it used to be that vehicles would pull into the lot, and when there would be nowhere to park, they would take their business to some other coffee shop.

But now, the lot can handle more cars at any given time. That means the coffee shop is doing more business—six more carloads at its busiest—which means one precedent-setting decision on how to park has rippled quite happily into the profit margin of this local coffee shop.

In the legal system, precedent-setting laws aren't just a function of human nature, where people unwittingly follow suit until a consistent pattern or routine is solidified. Rather, the concept of establishing and following legal precedent based on previous rulings and cases is one of the most important cornerstones in shaping American law. One would be hard-pressed to find a legal brief filed in any court that does not reference previous and similar cases to demonstrate existing legal precedent in trying to validate the brief's argument.

Legal precedent promotes uniformity and certainty within the judicial system. By adhering to established decisions, courts ensure that similar cases are treated comparably, thereby providing a predictable legal framework for individuals, businesses, and the government. This predictability is crucial for the effective functioning of society, as it allows people to plan their affairs with a reasonable expectation of legal outcomes.

There are multiple benefits for systems that legally prioritize precedent when considering new cases as they come before the Court. Precedent plays a pivotal role in the organic development of law, allowing it to evolve in response to changing societal values, technological advancements, and new challenges.

Landmark cases often introduce new legal principles or refine existing ones, thereby shaping the trajectory of legal thought and practice over time. For instance, landmark decisions in areas such as civil rights, privacy, and free speech have profoundly influenced American society and its legal landscape (we will discuss further as this chapter progresses).

Justices profit greatly from relying on precedent-setting legal cases. The reliance on precedent streamlines judicial decision-making by providing a framework for resolving cases. This efficiency is particularly important given the yearly influx of new cases courts must handle and adjudicate. By referring to established precedents, judges can resolve disputes more efficiently, reducing the need for extensive litigation on issues that have been previously addressed.

This benefit cannot be overstated. As our nation grows and we become a more litigious society (this is true for both civil and criminal trials), the caseload that justices are asked to navigate can be downright backbreaking.

Finally, legal precedents, especially those established by the Supreme Court, play a critical role in safeguarding individual rights and liberties. Landmark decisions have expanded and clarified constitutional protections, ensuring that fundamental rights are preserved and protected against infringement. Cases that have established significant precedents in areas such as equality, freedom of expression, and the right to privacy have had lasting impacts on American society.

Relying on established legal precedent is expedient, allows for consistency across multiple circuits, and does not require every case to be tried entirely from scratch. Yet, there are instances where leaning too heavily on precedent can cause a slightly askew previous ruling to inappropriately influence a case where a new ruling is necessary.

In previous chapters, I discussed at length the ineffectual way specific long-standing laws and arguments have been applied to social media. A rescan of that discussion will give you a better idea of how vital it is for the courts to reexamine how they are applying inaccurate laws of precedent to rulings focused on that ever-changing technology.

Simply put, when the courts won't offer a new ruling, and rely instead on the misapplication of landmark rulings as precedent, the law is being stunted when compared to the explosive growth of complex issues in our society. Establishing a new precedent is required, as it has the power to shape law in a way that betters society.

Conversely, when a case is denied based on old or misaligned precedent, a justice is effectively shaping the law as well—because the next time that issue is tried, that dismissal may be used to explain why something does not deserve space on the docket. As is true with most things in our justice system, the same things that have made our country such a bastion of freedom can be flipped on their heads and misused in ways that stifle our ability to keep up with the changing times.

Landmark Cases—We'd Be Lost Without Them

If you drive south from Covington, Kentucky, you'll soon begin seeing signs directing you toward the various famous distilleries in the area. Not far outside of Lexington, you'll be drawn to a place called Bardstown. This small town, boasting a population of not quite fourteen thousand, is one of the oldest towns in all of Kentucky and has been the center of the bourbon industry for almost as long as the industry has been in existence.

For most people in my neck of the woods, if you know how to get to Bardstown, you're not lost. If you can find Bardstown, then you can get home. More importantly, if you can find Bardstown, you can discover the distilleries of Heaven Hill, Buffalo Trace, Four Roses, and Wild Turkey (to name just a few notable brands)—which means you're going to be just fine. To put it another way, Bardstown is one of the most important landmarks in all of Kentucky. It's a place around which physical navigation, bourbon lore, Kentucky history, and even Western Expansion orbit.

In the United States legal system, landmark cases have significantly shaped the landscape by establishing important precedents. These cases have addressed a wide range of issues, from civil rights to federal powers, and have profoundly impacted American law and society at large.

One of the reasons landmark cases exist in our legal system is the doctrine of *stare decisis*. Stare decisis, meaning in Latin "to stand by things decided," is a legal principle that directs courts to adhere to previous judgments (or judgments of higher courts) while resolving a case with allegedly comparable facts.

The concept of stare decisis has two primary components: horizontal and vertical. Horizontal stare decisis refers to how, with the exception of extraordinary circumstances, a court will follow its previous decisions. On the other hand, vertical stare decisis speaks to the obligations that lower courts have to adhere strictly to decisions made by jurisdictionally higher courts. For example, a federal court of appeals must abide by decisions made by the U.S. Supreme Court.

These landmark cases aren't just obscure rulings that are referenced in courtrooms, or off the record in a judge's chambers. These are rulings with which ordinary, everyday citizens with absolutely zero experience in law are almost expertly familiar. Here are just a few examples of landmark cases that have changed the legal and social landscape of our country:

> *Marbury v. Madison* (1803): Established the principle of judicial review, allowing the Supreme Court to declare laws unconstitutional, thus affirming the

judiciary's role as a co-equal branch of government.

McCulloch v. Maryland (1819): Confirmed the federal government's implied powers under the Necessary and Proper Clause and asserted federal supremacy over state laws, particularly ruling that states cannot tax the federal government.

Dred Scott v. Sandford (1857): Ruled that African Americans, whether free or slaves, could not be American citizens and, therefore, had no standing to sue in federal court. Happily, this decision was later nullified by the 13th and 14th Amendments. The nullification of this verdict is a beautiful example of how the application of law and the passing of new legislation can exist for the betterment of our society.

Brown v. Board of Education (1954): Declared racial segregation in public schools unconstitutional, overturning the "separate but equal" doctrine established by *Plessy v. Ferguson*.

Miranda v. Arizona (1966): Established that detained criminal suspects must be informed of their right to an attorney and against self-incrimination prior to police questioning, leading to the implementation of the "Miranda Rights."

Roe v. Wade (1973): Legalized abortion nationwide, asserting that the right to privacy under the Due Process Clause of the 14th Amendment extends to a woman's decision to have an abortion. While this was recently overturned, it's almost impossible to find a relatively knowledgeable person in our country who has not heard of this and can reference it, if even at a surface-level understanding. And there is *Dobbs v. Jackson Women's Health Organization*, the 2022 decision that reversed the *Roe* decision.

Texas v. Johnson (1989): Ruled that flag burning constitutes symbolic speech that is protected by the First Amendment.

District of Columbia v. Heller (2008): Held that the Second Amendment protects an individual's right to possess a firearm for traditionally lawful purposes, such as self-defense within the home.

Obergefell v. Hodges (2015): The 2015 Supreme Court decision that guaranteed same-sex couples the right to marry.

Of course, as we have discussed, there is the *New York Times v. Sullivan* case. This 1964 Supreme Court decision changed the traditional approach to defamation and added a requirement that a public official must prove that a false and defamatory statement was published with actual malice to hold a publisher liable for a defamatory comment.

A brief look at this list, and you will see a few topics which are still as relevant in today's society as they've ever been. *Brown v. Board of Education* has been referenced in countless movies (from gritty dramas to uplifting sports films). Search "Miranda Rights" on YouTube, and you can spend the better part of a day scrolling through a number of videos, ranging from explanations of the concept to real-time examples of when law enforcement got it right (or wrong).

I would be remiss if I didn't pause for a moment on *Roe vs. Wade*, given the Supreme Court's latest ruling, which gave the decision regarding abortion back to each state—opening the door for states to allow, limit, or ban the practice completely. I will not get into my personal beliefs on the matter of abortion —that's a topic for a different book altogether—but the fact that the Supreme Court initially heard the challenge, and then ruled to overturn a landmark case that has stood for nearly fifty years, is a pertinent example of how the laws of our land can evolve as our nation grows.

I do not believe that landmark cases were ever meant to stand for time immemorial. Again, *Dread Scott v. Stanford* is a perfect example of how a growing nation was able to right a legal wrong by not only overturning a landmark case, but then enacting amendments to our Constitution which resolved the matter once and for all. When it comes to defamation, and the various ways a person's right to a good reputation is being assaulted (whether it's through new technologies the likes of which could not have been conceived when initial defamation legislation was formed, or the misapplication of laws that we discussed in Chapter eight), we are in desperate need of new landmark rulings.

Instead, I'm seeing an alarming trend toward two different reactions to defamation suits: dismissals based on previous precedent, or settlements (either at the request of the defending party to cover up their wrongful behavior, or at the behest of the presiding judge). Either way, we need to find new ways of bringing these cases before a jury.

Sad to Settle

If a case is not initially dismissed by a judge, it is likely on course for one of two outcomes. The parties reach a settlement (either prior to the trial starting, or once the trial has begun—although in defamation cases, a settlement after the trial has started is rare), or the case goes to trial, and a ruling is eventually rendered. It may seem elementary to some, but it's worth taking a moment to look at the differences between a settlement and a ruling.

Settlements are agreements reached between disputing parties without a trial or a judicial ruling. They are often negotiated privately and can involve compromises by both sides. Because they are private agreements and often do not involve a detailed examination of legal principles, settlements do not contribute to the body of case law that guides future judicial decisions—that is to say, settlements do not create legal precedent for future cases.

One of the key components of settlements is that they are often confidential and not part of the public record, which can limit public knowledge about the case and its resolution. Lastly, settlements are final agreements that typically preclude further litigation on the matter between the parties (barring breaches of the settlement terms).

Rulings, on the other hand, are decisions made by a judge or a jury at the conclusion of a trial. They are based on the application of law to the facts presented during the trial. Importantly, rulings, especially those from appellate courts, establish legal precedents that bind future cases. This contributes to the development of the law and provides a framework for resolving similar disputes.

Since rulings come from a full trial, they are public and contribute to the transparency of the judicial process. They allow the public to understand how decisions are made, and the legal reasoning behind them. Finally, rulings can often be appealed to a higher court, which can review the decision for errors in law or procedure.

For many lawyers, corporations, and judges, settlements are often a preferred outcome for most cases. As I discussed earlier, there is a high value on expediency in our court system. In almost every instance, this is not due to laziness. Rather, when a case can be resolved through settlement, it often demonstrates that the two opposing parties have found a middle ground, allows for a fast resolution without tying up valuable judicial resources, and frequently saves both parties from massive amounts in legal fees and public relations nightmares.

The issue, however, is that there are situations that be brought to light. There are cases that require a full understanding of the wrongs perpetrated against an innocent person. There are times when the law must weigh in, or be shaped. And when these types of cases are settled, our nation suffers a gravely missed opportunity. We must keep in mind that, regardless of whether a case is settled or a ruling is handed down, there is an impact on the judicial landscape either way:

Impact on Justice and Fairness:

- Settlements can raise questions of justice and fairness, as they may not always reflect the merits of the case but rather the negotiating power of the parties. This can sometimes result in outcomes that deviate from what might have been decided based on legal principles alone.

- Rulings are based on legal merits and ensure that decisions are made according to established laws and precedents, which can be seen as a more objective measure of justice.

Role of Judges:

- Judges play a significant role in encouraging settlements as a means to resolve disputes efficiently and reduce court backlogs. However, excessive judicial involvement in settlements can raise concerns about impartiality and the pressure on parties to settle.

- In issuing rulings, judges apply legal principles to the facts of the case, contributing to the development of the law and ensuring that decisions are made within the framework of existing legal standards.

Effect on Legal Precedent:

- Settlements do not contribute to the development of legal precedent, which can limit the evolution of the law in certain areas.

- Rulings create precedents that guide future judicial decisions, contributing to the consistency and predictability of the law.

Settlements are one thing. Dismissals from judges are something entirely different. When a case is settled, it's because both sides have looked at all of the filings and arguments, and decide, based on all available information, the best course of action. In defamation cases, the defendants (the people or corporations who acted in a defamatory way) will want to avoid all of the evidence going public, and will certainly not want to leave their fate to a jury. If they can settle with the plaintiff, they will almost certainly do so (albeit for a drastically reduced sum).

Why would the plaintiff (the person defamed) be willing to settle? In most cases (as I discussed in previous chapters), the incentive here is to avoid costly legal fees and a lengthy trial that most everyday citizens don't have the time or resources to attend. It also insulates them from ultimately losing the trial. Often, a party believes "a bird in the hand is better than two in the bush," and settles to assure themselves of a positive result. Some cases are very strong and can generate sizable settlements. In this circumstance, there is just too much money on the table to gamble with losing it.

But even when a case is settled for a smaller sum, the plaintiff usually walks away with some sort of financial restitution. Some settlements are for smaller dollar amounts because the case has a flaw or two, which makes success in a trial uncertain. These instances, however, are almost always bittersweet for my clients, because the victory feels hollow. There is almost always a wrong that has occurred, but it is hard to hold the responsible party to account. Along with a settlement usually comes some sort of non-disclosure agreement, where both parties are bound to not speak publicly about the case ever again under penalty of having the settlement nullified.

It's the adult version of getting beat up by a bully who happens to be the principal's child, being sent to the nurse's office, and being offered a lollipop. While the lollipop may distract momentarily from your throbbing nose, you will still have a black eye the next day, and the bully will have moved on to his next victim.

Worse still, when a case is dismissed, either at the outset or upon appeal, if the initial ruling was not favorable to the plaintiff, there is absolutely no recompense for the victim of the defamation. The bully keeps being the bully, and you don't even get to have your wounds tended by the nurse, let alone receive a fleeting sugary treat.

Either way, the bully gets to continue roaming around, harming anyone unlucky enough to cross his path.

If you've ever seen me in an interview talking about these topics, you will hear me repeat this refrain almost every single time: "Nick Sandmann deserved his day in court." He deserved to look the leaders of those smug, irresponsible, and ideologically compromised corporations in the eyes as he detailed how he'd been irreparably harmed by them. And those goons deserved to have a jury hear how unethically they approach their role as arbiters of truth in our society. And it doesn't stop at Nick. Friends and victims of defamation deserve their day in court as often as possible.

I'm glad that Nick was able to settle with a couple of the media conglomerates. However, many of the worst offenders stubbornly dug their heels into the sand and refused to settle. Being confident in how defamation law for so long has been molded to protect the media, the media defendants were indignant about being sued. Their attorneys could not have cared less about what their clients had done. One of the lawyers always seemed to find what happened to Nick to be funny. It was just a joke, a game. I wonder what this person would think if it had happened to their child. To them, the press and news organizations were the protectors of democracy. These lawyers and their clients were as blind to the lies their clients published as the gullible audiences that get their news from MSNBC. The whole crowd, sadly, lacks intellectual curiosity. Instead, they are just perched on what they think is the moral high ground. They see themselves as guardians of the dominant culture. But for me, a person my wife calls a rebel and non-conformist, I could barely mask my disdain at their condescension. I knew I was right, and they were wrong. That they did not know this rendered what they thought about me to be meaningless. But I did not get angry. To me, it was just a manifestation of a society that is off course.

These folks consume the drivel of the liberal news, and media organizations spoon-feed them without thought or criticism. Now, please don't get me wrong. Fox News is every bit as bad as CNN. But if you care, less biased and more truthful sources of news do exist. Most people, however, just don't care. I will admit—the fact that highly educated people obviously did not care was troubling. If these guardians of elite sensibility did not care about what happened to a 16-year-old kid, what would they think about a less vulnerable victim? All you need to do is look at what happened to the poor folks who foolishly entered our nation's Capitol on January 6, 2021. Just consider the glee that is so easily detected when a conservative is canceled. It's an atheist's version of an animal sacrifice. It is cathartic and religious for progressives.

As for the judges who passed judgment on Nick's case (a judgment I think is obviously wrong), they, too, saw a reality in stark contrast to what I see to be right. I saw a travesty of news reporting; they saw just the news. It is unfortunate that the judges in Nick's case (again, acting as aged gatekeepers and applying outdated precedential case law, designed to protect news organizations to maintain freedom of press and expression) decided to dismiss Nick's case. They should have understood that Nick's case was different. It came at a time when the press had abandoned its principles and no longer deserved the protections decades of law provided. The rulings in Nick's case were missed opportunities to rebalance the scales to protect innocent victims of inflamed cancel culture. I often thought, "Surely this judge will see the truth of what's going on. Certainly, this panel of judges will understand the importance of applying the case law in updated ways to temper press overreach. How can the courts defend multibillion-dollar media entities that behaved so badly? Of course, the Supreme Court will understand the necessity of progress when it comes to defamation."

Not so. It seems we are still winding our way through the dark valley when it comes to protecting ourselves against cancel culture and outdated legal standards.

What would I have liked to see happen? Because I care about Nick, I wanted to see him win in a trial decided by his peers. Yes, the monetary award would have been great for him. Even better, it would have aided in healing the wounds he suffered by having a group of twelve people stand up and confirm that he's not alone—there are reasonable people in this nation, and we're not puppets to be manipulated by the whims of extremism. Nick's an incredibly strong person, and he's overcome so much since that day on the steps of the Lincoln Memorial—but a win would have been sweet.

On a larger scale, Nick needed his day in court so attacks like this stop. I have no doubt that if his case had gone to trial, we would have had a big win. And in winning, we would have been able to add one more landmark case to the list I offered earlier in this chapter. And with that landmark, I believe we would begin to see the media and those on the extreme Left be held to account more often. Ultimately, I think we would begin to see less of these ever-intensifying media hit jobs.

Trimming the Legal Hedges

I'm not one who is usually given to flights of fancy. There are enough real and tangible causes on which to spend my time. I also realize that changes to defamation law will likely not come as part of a tsunami that crashes onshore and wipes the slate clean. But as I look at how these cases are handled, I can't help but imagine a few key areas that would significantly change the landscape for the better. Balancing settlements and legal precedent in defamation cases requires a multifaceted approach that considers the interests of both parties involved in the dispute, as well as the broader goals of the legal system.

The following is a list of changes I think would alter the landscape of defamation law, so that the media and large corporations would think twice before acting as inappropriately as they do now.

One of the most important changes I would make is to the anti-SLAPP laws, which have been purloined from their original intent and are being used to embolden those in the press who most frequently engage in defamatory attacks.

Modify Anti-SLAPP Laws: Originally created to stop frivolous and irresponsible lawsuits, anti-SLAPP (short for Strategic Lawsuits Against Public Participation) laws force the plaintiffs to pay the legal fees of the defendants should the plaintiff not prevail. For example, if you sue a major newspaper for defamation of character and lose, you could be required to pay the legal fees they incurred. And because most media outlets have enormous teams of lawyers, their legal fees are exorbitant. In essence, anti-SLAPP laws are tantamount to intimidation.

Initially aimed to prevent the misuse of courts to intimidate those exercising their First Amendment rights, these laws have played a crucial role in safeguarding free speech and preventing powerful entities from using lawsuits to silence critics through costly and meritless litigation. This sounds great, but over time, anti-SLAPP has become another barrier for everyday citizens in recent years. Companies have now started using anti-SLAPP as a deterrent to prevent individuals from initiating a valid case unless they want to risk paying all the fees if they lose.

Designed at first to be used as a shield for the "Davids" of the world, it now has become a close combat dagger for the "Goliaths." This is especially damaging to people who are wrongly drawn into controversy and have their lives ruined. Not only are they robbed of their good name, but they are told that if they attempt to put up a fight, they run the risk of being financially ruined. It is almost cruel to add this burden to someone who may have just lost their job, business, or prospects for the future. But today, that is what the law does.

For this reason, plaintiffs often choose to sue media defendants in Delaware because it does not have an anti-SLAPP law. As an example from an earlier chapter, H.A. (the child Deadspin defamed) filed his suit in Delaware because Deadspin's parent company was incorporated in Delaware, making this state an appropriate jurisdiction for H.A. to pursue his claims.

Simply put, anti-SLAPP laws shouldn't apply to private individuals. If you're not famous and a local paper publishes a lie about you, you shouldn't risk financial ruin to protect your reputation.

Make it Easier to Sue for Defamation

Let's start by changing the rule that requires public figures to prove *actual malice* when suing for defamation. When it comes to defamatory statements, it is virtually impossible to prove actual malice because we can't read the mind of the person who is defaming another. Might there be some sort of litmus test that could better identify intent? We have this in other areas of the law—when deciding between first and second-degree murder, for example, we must look at intent through things like whether the death was pre-planned or in self-defense.

This will make it easier for them to protect their reputations. After all, the media are powerful, multibillion-dollar corporations—so they can handle the lawsuits. Plus, it will make journalists more careful about what they write, improve public discourse, and possibly reduce the hyper-partisan news cycle. Honestly, I'm surprised the Supreme Court hasn't done this already.

The Supreme Court should also change the rule that limits where you can sue for defamation. Currently, if someone in California writes something defamatory about you, you usually have to sue them in California. It would be much easier and fairer if you could sue them in your own state. This change could help reduce defamation and cancel culture.

Beginning in high school, everyone should take a course on online behavior. This would help people understand the real-world effects of attacking someone online, and teach them how to protect their reputations. Future journalists would go to college with a better understanding of the negative aspects of online defamation and cancellation.

We should also make it a crime to dox or cancel someone online, especially if they're a minor. Kentucky has already passed a law like this, thanks to Nick Sandmann, and other states should follow suit.

Judicial Changes

Judges should no longer decide if a statement is a fact or opinion. The Constitution guarantees the right to a jury trial, and that right shouldn't be overridden to protect the press. Let a jury decide if a statement is a fact or opinion. In many ways, taking this decision out of the hands of a jury has placed the press in a new type of "protected class" that can operate outside of the law. As the popular saying goes, Power corrupts—and absolute power corrupts absolutely.

Currently, if a newspaper publishes a defamatory article, you have one year to sue. However, with online articles, which can stay online forever, this isn't fair. We should change the law so that you can sue for as long as the defamatory article is online.

Just as left-leaning billionaires support their causes, conservative billionaires should fund defamation cases. Over time, this could shape the law to better protect the average American from defamation and cancellation.

Legislative and Regulatory Reforms

To discourage the press from irresponsible reporting, states should allow successful defamation plaintiffs to recover triple damages and attorney fees. This change would protect the average citizen from defamation and cancellation, similar to laws for commercial disputes and racketeering.

Congress should set legal standards for defamation that include the suggestions outlined here. Many states already have uniform laws on various issues, and the federal government should do the same for defamation.

Congress should also change Section 230 of the Communications Decency Act, which currently gives social media companies immunity for what users post. Many voices on Capitol Hill are already calling for this change. The combination of current defamation laws, anti-SLAPP laws, and Section 230 gives too much protection to those who engage in defamation and cancellation.

Public Engagement and Advocacy

We need public engagement and advocacy to raise awareness about the importance of protecting reputations. This book aims to arm you with the knowledge to defend your reputation, and a charitable foundation could do the same.

Encourage dialogue between legal experts, media organizations, and civil society groups to find ways to reduce defamation and cancel culture. Average Americans need protection, but so far, the courts have been more interested in protecting biased media organizations. Advocacy could help by urging social media companies and news organizations to implement better protections against defamation and cancellation.

Weary, Yet Hopeful

There are benefits and drawbacks to almost every item I just listed. And if you talk to other lawyers fighting on the frontlines of defamation law, they would most certainly add substantive and innovative options as well. But that's the point —defamation law is ripe with the opportunity to be updated in a way that benefits every aspect of our society. Folks, the mountain in front of us is considerable—the Army on the other side is formidable. But I, for one, have never been more motivated to keep climbing and fighting. We have to. The consequences of not fighting are too dire.

We previously reviewed the case where a child was attacked by Deadspin for how he chose to cheer for his team in a way that fully aligned with team culture. At the time of this book's publication, that case is still in its infancy. However, I'm ecstatic that a case is being brought. And, on some level, I desperately hope they do not choose to settle the matter without a trial. Instead, I hope they play the role of the blue Ford Ranger at the coffee shop. I can see the dynamics of the defamatory parking lot starting to shift. Each time we file a complaint and name a defendant for outlandish and improper defamation, another car pulls in nose-to-curb. Eventually, a precedent will be set—it's only a matter of time—and I can't help but think that Nick will be somewhere nearby, standing resolutely with a comfortable smile on his face.

WE MUST WIN

STANDING STRONG FOR OUR FUTURE

"The great enemy of the truth is very often not the lie, deliberate,
contrived and dishonest, but the myth, persistent,
persuasive and unrealistic."
- John F. Kennedy

There is a defining battle in every generation. In the 1950s, racial issues grew so tense that the status quo of segregation and other divisive laws could no longer be sustained, which ultimately led to the *Brown vs. Board of Education* ruling. While this by no means solved racial tension in our country, it was a seminal moment of progress for how we moved forward as a nation.

The 1960s saw citizens crying out against wars halfway across the world, and how our military engaged in those conflicts. Financial crises, gas lines, and poverty, the likes of which hadn't been seen since the Depression, caused an incredible amount of distrust and frustration toward our government in the 1970s. And in the 1980s, a deadly, fast-spreading virus swept the world in the form of AIDS. While people fought with the realities of a new virus, they once again grew angry toward the government for the way it was handling the care for those impacted.

Racial issues, wars, financial crises, and the government's response to a new disease—as we find ourselves forging into the second quarter of the 21st century, it's as if many of our past woes have been resurrected once again. However, the crucial issue exacerbating everything else truly seems to be the constant re-writing of what is "Right" or "Wrong," and the swift attack, judgment, and retribution from those pushing their ideological worldview through the brutal application of cancel culture toward anyone who might step out of line.

Standing strong against defamatory cancel culture and forced compliance may well be this generation's most important fight. I don't say this because it's the battle in which I'm embroiled. Rather, if I look at the things that are shaping our culture, I'm hard-pressed to find another topic as salient as this one. When we are made to fear being attacked when we don't vote for the Mob's candidate, or say the thing the media has decided is the right thing to say, we no longer live in the Land of the Free and Home of the Brave.

We find ourselves in a delicate situation. We can't just go "scorched earth" in how we battle this mindset because sadly, we're too far down the wrong path. Just like a Spanish 101 teacher can't just walk into her room on the first day of class and begin speaking only Spanish, she has to lead her students down a careful path, helping them understand verb conjugation, sentence structure, and key vocabulary.

Many have been taught the wrong vocabulary required to live in the United States, and we need to help "unteach" some of the wrong information that has been taught as canon. In short, we need to be strategic in how we fight this battle.

Let's Pull Together

I can't help but recall a case my dad was trying when I was a kid. The details of the case aren't important—the city was being sued for something, and my father was the City Attorney. As the trial loomed closer and closer, it became apparent that the opposing counsel didn't really have much of a case. My father was too prepared, and the case was shaky to begin with.

On the day of the trial, the attorney for the plaintiff called in sick, claiming to have the flu, and asked for a few more days in order to "get better." My father, upon hearing this, and being an incredibly savvy and strategic person, had the feeling that something strange was going on. Trusting his gut, he called a local private investigator to track down the lawyer to ensure he had the flu. Turns out, my dad's hunch was right. The investigator reported back to my father with pictures of the lawyer going to the grocery store, attending his kid's baseball game, and a variety of other things that a person with the flu would not be doing.

Armed with the photographs and details from the private investigator, he called a meeting. Once he'd laid out the evidence to the opposing lawyer, which proved that he'd lied to the court, it wasn't long before the lawyer agreed to settle the case. My dad had saved the court countless hours of hearings, and had gained a favorable settlement for his client. It wasn't a traditional way of winning a case, but it was clever, and it got the job done against an opposing attorney who had already proven to be willing to lie to get what he wanted. My dad found the best winning option.

What does that look like for us as we fight to claw our way out from under outdated laws, gigantic corporations, and a media that has lost its ethical compass? My first thought goes to the parents of Loudoun County.

In 2021, a video out of Loudoun County, Virginia, began circulating of a father being arrested at a school board meeting. At first, the typical uneducated hit job from the extreme Left went into full swing. The father was framed as the face of an anti-LGBTQIA+ parental group that was trying to intimidate the board from enacting racial and equity plans. However, as more information regarding the meeting came to light, it became clear this was a very different situation.

The man being arrested was nothing like how he was being portrayed. In fact, his daughter had been raped by a student who described himself as "gender-fluid." The rape occurred in the girl's restroom, which the gender-fluid boy had been allowed to enter due to the school's transgender policy. The scene at the school board meeting, which was caught on video, occurred when the superintendent denied that there was a record of the assault. [1]The father in question, as any father in that situation, would not stand for such a lie and was subsequently arrested.

If the rape wasn't bad enough, the ensuing investigation revealed a shocking level of administration and staff misconduct—lies, cover-ups, and even evidence that a teacher had been in the restroom during the assault, seen two sets of feet in a stall, but did nothing to stop what was happening. The gender-fluid boy later admitted that the restroom was the perfect place for such an attack because even if teachers went in and saw two sets of feet, they wouldn't do anything.

These details are nothing short of horrific. I can't imagine any parent acting differently upon uncovering such information. These things should not be the reality of our society. However, the policies of Loudoun County Public

Schools and the negligence of the school staff allowed truly despicable things to happen to innocent children.

As we've seen from almost all of the case studies in the book, the process was similar. There was no help from the legal system. The media was largely complicit in the cover-up, until they could no longer keep control of the narrative. The parents in the school district were left to fend for themselves.

This is where inspiration comes in. The parents rallied together and took the school district to task on every front.

Parents filed lawsuits against Loudoun County Public Schools over racial equity plans and a biased reporting system, claiming these initiatives violated students' First Amendment rights and discriminated against students based on race. A federal judge initially dismissed the lawsuit regarding racial equity plans, ruling that the parents failed to show that the school system's guidance violated First Amendment rights. However, the controversy over the biased reporting system led to a federal court hearing, with parents arguing that the policy stifles free speech.

Due to the light that the parents shined on the terrible way in which the school board handled the assault, the school board faced calls for resignation, and the superintendent at the time, Scott Ziegler, was fired. A special grand jury investigation was initiated by Governor Glenn Youngkin, leading to indictments against Ziegler and a school spokesperson.

Unwilling to stop there, Loudoun County parents have fueled a broader parental rights movement, with Governor Glenn Youngkin pardoning the father who was arrested at that first school board meeting following his daughter's sexual assault. This movement has focused on increasing parental involvement in education and challenging policies perceived as infringing on parents' rights to guide their children's education. Ultimately, some of these same parents got elected to the school board by promising changes in policies and approaches to address parents' concerns.

Others across the nation have taken notice. We are seeing more and more school board members who have been quietly shaping pro-woke curriculum and policy, challenged in local elections—and the challengers who stand for parent's rights and refuse to bow to the woke mob are winning. There's a groundswell that is finally addressing issues that have been allowed to lie hidden for far too long.

This brings hope, but it hardly scratches the surface across this nation. The same changes are needed across all levels of government, in corporate boardrooms, and in how we hold news media to account. Ultimately, we need better legislation. We need new landmark rulings, which means we need judges who will let these cases go to trial. But if the legal system is going to drag its feet, we must engage at every level possible. It's happening, and I'm encouraged by how resolute so many are already proving to be.

Defying the Odds

I'm reminded of the film *Defiance*, starring Daniel Craig. The film is based on a true story of World War II, and portrays how a group of roughly one thousand Jews were able to escape German-occupied Eastern Europe and build a hidden community in the Belorussian forest. It is a gritty film that details the trials of the community while the world is shrinking around them as the Nazis grow closer and closer to finding and eradicating the group. In the film, Daniel Craig leads a band of fighters dedicated to protecting the larger group from roaming bands of Nazis, building structures, and providing some level of organization so the community does not implode on itself.

In a crucial scene of the film, Daniel Craig's character is talking to another leader who advocates that they would be a stronger community if they were to eliminate the older and weaker people. Craig pauses, then with stirring clarity, says, "Our revenge is to live."[2] The implication is that, in the midst of the holocaust raging around them, the life of every person is precious. For the person Craig portrayed, every soul that survived the war was a victory.

For us in this battle against cancel culture, which props up so many devastating ideologies, the only way we lose is if we stop. Things can't keep going the way they have been. We're beginning to stand up and (regardless of whether we're like Matt Walsh and work for a company that has our backs) say, "Enough is enough." The only way this movement slips out of our grasp is if we quiet down.

A landmark precedent will be established. There will be a time when transparency and accountability will be the norm again—where a person's right to a good and true reputation will not be sacrificed so the media can push more and more control through ideology.

The path is daunting, but there's no other path I'd rather walk down, and no other battle I'd rather fight. Our nation needs this battle to be fought, and we must be the ones to win. If we don't keep fighting, the defining battle for the next generation may be for the nation itself.

Chapter Notes

1 Drew Wilder, Jackie Bensen, and Andrea Swalec, "'The Meeting Has Degenerated': 1 Arrest, 1 Injury at Loudoun Schools Meeting on Equity," last modified Jun 23, 2021, 2021, accessed May 24, 2024, https://www.nbcwashington.com/news/local/northern-virginia/loudoun-school-board-transgender-student-policy-race-equity/2708185/.

2 Defiance, (Paramount Pictures, 2008).

DON'T BE DISMISSED

WHAT TO DO WHEN YOU ARE IN THE CROSSHAIRS

Welcome to this modern age, where anyone can be a worldwide content publisher, and news outlets escalate sensationalism to try to make a buck. Combined with increasingly aggressive behaviors around intersectional issues, these factors create a world where the average American can suddenly be swept up into a larger narrative that seeks to victimize them for the benefit of money and agenda. Anyone can simply be minding their own business one moment, and then suddenly find themselves at the center of a local, state, or national issue.

I have represented college athletes, high school cheerleaders, and frightened parents involved in seemingly minor incidents that suddenly have the students suffering through Maoist struggle sessions, disciplinary actions, and expulsions. All are arising from literally nothing, that is recast as religiosity, racism, or one of the "phobias." The point is: this can happen to you.

Sadly, if you are a public figure, this potential for scrutiny is the price you pay for your service or notoriety. But if you are a private figure just trying to engage in life, liberty, and the pursuit of happiness, there are some things you can do. I have outlined some of them below based on situations you may face.

However, please note that the information below is intended only to serve as a foundation for the "rules of the game." These are not a substitute for legal advice and cannot be viewed as a cure-all recipe for anything. If you are embroiled in a defamation situation (or about to be), you should shut your mouth and consult a lawyer immediately.

Before Anything Ever Happens

- Maintain a private lifestyle, consider limiting your use of social media, and be mindful of the information you share online. Consider using privacy-focused platforms or minimizing your digital footprint by not sharing personal details.

- Be cautious about how you respond to public situations. If something is happening that you don't appreciate (like someone being noisy in a restaurant), consider leaving. We don't live in the old days when you can safely ask someone to quiet down and not have it blown out of proportion because of their sex, race, religion, or creed.

- Invest time and energy in building strong, face-to-face relationships with family and friends. Avoid unnecessary sharing or venting in public forums. These days, everyone listens and often makes video recordings. You do not need to live in fear, but it is good to be mindful.

- Use a service such as Super Lawyers or Martindale-Hubbell to identify an attorney in your community who understands defamation law. Not every attorney is familiar with the intricacies of this part of the legal realm, and you want to avoid scrambling at the last minute to find one.

When Something Happens

Maybe you are about to be defamed, or a reporter or coach (for example) has reached out to you, or the defamation has already occurred. Whatever the case may be, here are your first steps:

- Breathe and Remain Calm: Fear and anxiety of financial loss or reputational harm (for you or the people you care about) is powerful. You want to avoid making any unforced errors or taking precipitous action.

- Humble Yourself: You may want to get angry and aggressive (another fear-based response). You may think you can "win" by arguing and making yourself heard. You cannot. Fight this urge and remember the game is not to be understood; it is to make the truth clear enough in writing that the other party is liable for their behavior if they defame you. This is a significant difference. Also, recognize you can do everything right and still "lose."

- Get Help: Immediately contact the trusted people in your life for moral support and consult a good attorney familiar with defamation law.

- Keep Quiet: Holding your peace and not saying anything is okay. If you cannot afford a competent attorney, consider saying nothing to avoid compounding the injury. This is one of those situations where saying the wrong thing or responding in the wrong way can hurt you more than keeping quiet. Don't be drawn into the game of having to react immediately.

- In Writing: Communicate only in writing and retain all communications. You want to ensure a detailed written record of everything that has transpired.

If a Reporter Has Reached Out to You, or You Have Been Made Aware of an Upcoming News Story

It is important to remember that in these situations, you want to set a stage where the news outlet can be shown to publish information you already proved to them in writing was false. Once they know something is untrue, they are negligent in moving forward with the story. Here are some important principles to remember (in addition to those listed above):

- Watch What You Say: Do not speak with the reporter or consent to be recorded. Do not try to speak "off the record," as different journalists treat off-the-record conversations differently.

- Proactively Communicate in Writing: I have provided an example template below. This can be used later to establish actual malice, negligence, or reckless disregard, as they may apply. The idea is to set up a scenario in which it can be shown that the publication moved forward "with the knowledge that it was false or with reckless disregard for whether it was false or not."

- Inform Them: Let them know that you either intend to or have discussed the situation with legal counsel (if applicable).

- Provide Clarification or Corrections: Correct any and all factual inaccuracies in the reporter's understanding, as well as clear and concise information to correct any misunderstandings.

- Request to Review: Politely ask if you can review the quote or the section where you are mentioned before the story is published. While journalists are not obligated to allow this, some may be open to fact-checking or confirming details with you to ensure accuracy.

- Express Your Concerns: If you are worried about potential misrepresentation, express your concerns to the reporter and explain the potential impact of inaccuracies. Be specific about what you believe is being misrepresented.

(Optional, As Needed)

- Cease and Desist: Depending on your lawyer's advice, sending a formal cease and desist letter may be appropriate. This letter will outline the potential for defamation action if the story is published as is.

- Contact the Editor: If the reporter is unresponsive or unwilling to address your concerns, you may contact the editor or the publication's ombudsman. Explain the situation and your concern about being misrepresented.

- Public Relations: Consider preparing a public statement or press release to respond to the story post-publication. This can help control the narrative and present your side of the story. If you have an online presence, be ready to update your social media with your response or clarification to mitigate reputational damage.

Here is a sample letter you could use:

Dear Addressee:

Your recent email suggests (their stated interpretation or mischaracterization). A plain review of (the writing or evidence in question) communicates nothing of the sort. My position is: (State your position clearly and succinctly).

I have consulted with a defamation attorney whom I intend to hire if you move forward with these mischaracterizations. My private comments regarding this situation are just that. I am not a public figure; this is not a matter of public concern, and sharing my private comments about (The Topic) intrudes upon my privacy. Even though I am a private figure, your statements about me are false. By virtue of this communication, you now know your characterization of my letter is false and defamatory.

(The Other Parties) should also understand that exposing my private communications to (him/her) violates my right to privacy and has already caused me and my family to suffer emotional distress and anxiety. Your decision to expose this private communication and, worse, to mischaracterize it is outrageous. I demand that you keep my affairs private and not expose me wrongfully to public hatred, ridicule, and contempt.

Sincerely,

Your Name

Don't Be Dismissed

If you have read the rest of the book, then you know that we are still in a time when the law is struggling to catch up with the fast pace of our lives today. You also know that sometimes the "bad guys" still win. People's good names are destroyed, lives are canceled, and political/media agendas sacrifice the lives of citizens on the altar of money or agenda. The guidelines I have outlined above are not a magic wand that will save you. Sadly, some people follow the rules perfectly and still lose either in court or public opinion. But that is why I do what I do, and why it is so important to shine a light on what is going on, and know what we can do about it.

It is my hope that you and your loved ones never need to use this guide, reach out to my office, or suffer the fear, anxiety, and loss that comes from being defamed or canceled. I still have hope that this great nation will recognize the need to change the laws and once again put the ability to protect our reputations back into the hands of the American people.

GLOSSARY OF IMPORTANT TERMS

actual malice: represents the defamatory standard established in *NYT V Sullivan*. It means that the defendant said the defamatory statement "with knowledge that it was false or with reckless disregard of whether it was false or not." This is often very difficult to prove.

amicus curiae briefs: literally translated from Latin, is "friend of the court." Plural is "amici curiae." Generally, it is referencing a person or group who is not a party to an action but has a strong interest in the matter. This person or group will petition the court for permission to submit a brief in the action intending to influence the court's decision. Such briefs are called "amicus briefs."

anti-SLAPP laws: originally created to stop frivolous and irresponsible lawsuits, anti-SLAPP (short for Strategic Lawsuits Against Public Participation) laws force the plaintiffs to pay the legal fees of the defendants should the plaintiff not prevail. The majority of states have these laws, and details vary. The choice of a case location can have a dramatic impact on whether these laws apply, and to what extent.

common law: law that is derived from judicial decisions instead of from statutes.

defamation: the act of communicating false statements about a person that injure the reputation of that person (sourced from

Merriam-Webster's dictionary, and referenced in the early chapters of this book).

defamatory per se: statements that are so obviously degrading or pernicious that no consideration of context or proof of reputational harm is required.

defendant: a person or group against whom legal action is brought by a plaintiff: someone who is being sued or accused.

deplatform: to prohibit a person, or a group of people, from sharing their views in a forum. This can be a public forum or one controlled by a third party, as in the case of social media websites or applications.

lawfare: in this work, it is the use of legal action by one person/ party to create social, financial, and personal challenges for an opponent. In many cases, it represents abusive and unjust uses of the law and often requires a complicit judge to be effective.

libel: a false statement that defames another person, expressed by print, writing, pictures, signs, effigies, or any communication embodied in physical form.

libel-proof defendant: in this work, it is defined as someone who has a public image so rooted in hyperbole, political discourse, or entertainment that nothing they say can be taken seriously.

libel-proof plaintiff: used in defamation cases to describe someone with no reputation to protect. That is, someone who, for one reason or another, has no "good name" that can be besmirched and, therefore, cannot claim to have a reputation that has been injured.

limited-purpose public figure: someone who is not considered a public figure generally, but interjects or participates in a public controversy/topic to the point where they may influence the outcome of that controversy. In the modern era, participating in social media can be enough to earn an individual this designation.

nuclear verdict: a verdict in favor of the plaintiff with an award surpassing $10 million, but the term is also frequently used to describe an outcome significantly surpassing anyone's expectations.

obloquy: a legal term for disgrace; it is often linked to disgrace that is associated with public abuse.

opinion defense: sometimes called "absolute defense," it is a legal principle that holds that statements made as opinions are protected speech and, therefore, can never be the basis of a defamation claim.

plaintiff: the party who initiates a lawsuit, bringing a case against another party.

presumed damages: sometimes also called "assumed damages," they are, in the eyes of the law, the necessary result from the publication of some kinds of defamatory matter. In other words, even if the plaintiff is unable to prove actual damages, the court can assume that a person suffered harm to their reputation (or some other loss).

punitive damages: also known as exemplary damages, these are awarded separately from the actual damages from an event. Generally awarded when it is determined that the defendant has acted in a particularly harmful way.

question of law: an issue that is always, and must be, resolved by a judge, not a jury of peers.

reputational harm/damage: occurs when false or harmful statements are made about an individual, business, or organization, leading to a tarnished reputation. While this damage can result in loss of finances, opportunities, relationships, and even emotional health, it is very difficult to quantify. This harm is considered perpetual when it impacts an individual, business, or organization for the remainder of its existence.

slander: a false statement, usually made orally, which defames another person.

stare decisis: meaning in Latin "to stand by things decided," a legal principle that directs courts to adhere to previous judgments (or judgments of higher courts) while resolving a case with allegedly comparable facts. There are two components to this:

- *horizontal* stare decisis: refers to a court adhering to its own precedent. A court adhering to the principle of horizontal stare decisis will follow its own prior decisions absent exceptional circumstances.

- *vertical* stare decisis: obligates lower courts to adhere strictly to rulings made by higher courts within the same jurisdiction.

BIBLIOGRAPHY

"About Acs." American Constitution Society. 2024. Accessed May 24, 2024. https://www.acslaw.org/about-us/.

"About Blexit." 2024. Accessed May 24, 2024. https://www.blexit.com/about.

"About Blexit." Blexit. Accessed May 24, 2024. https://www.blexit.com/about.

"About Us." The 65 Project. 2023. Accessed May 24, 2024. https://the65project.com/about/.

"About Us." Federalist Society. 2024. Accessed May 24, 2024. https://fedsoc.org/about-us#Background.

"Audrie Pott Suicide: Three Teens Arrested for Alleged Sexual Assault of Calif. Girl Who Committed Suicide." Last modified Apr 12, 2013, 2013. Accessed May 24, 2024. https://www.cbsnews.com/news/audrie-pott-suicide-three-teens-arrested-for-alleged-sexual-assault-of-calif-girl-who-committed-suicide/.

"Clare Locke Llp." 2024. Accessed May 24, 2024. https://clarelocke.com/.

"Healing the Soul of America." 2024. Accessed May 24, 2024. https://democrats.org/where-we-stand/party-platform/healing-the-soul-of-america/.

"Imagining the Internet's Quick Look at the Early History of the Internet." Elon University. Accessed May 2024, 2024. https://www.elon.edu/u/imagining/time-capsule/early-90s/internet-history/.

"Jon Stewart Tangles with Cnn's crossfire." 2004. Accessed May 24, 2024. https://bradt.ca/blog/jon-stewart-tangles-with-cnn-crossfire/.

"Literary Agent Fired for Joining Parler Tells Her Story." *New Tolerance Campaign*, May 242024. https://newtolerance.org/literary-agent-fired-for-joining-parler-tells-her-story/.

"Native American Elder Mocked by Young Donald Trump Supporters in Maga Hats? It's Not That Simple." ABC News. Last modified Sun 20 Jan 2019, 2019. Accessed May 24, 2024. https://www.abc.net.au/news/2019-01-21/native-american-surrounded-maga-trump-supporters-what-happened/10730988.

"New York Times V. Sullivan (1964)." Jack Miller Center. Accessed May 24, 2024. https://jackmillercenter.org/cd-resources/new-york-times-v-sullivan-1964/.

"Peter Navarro Indicted for Contempt of Congress." United States Attorney's Office (District of Columbia). Last modified June 3, 2022, 2022. Accessed May 24, 2024. https://www.justice.gov/usao-dc/pr/peter-navarro-indicted-contempt-congress.

"Rep. Massie Defends Cov Cath Students: 'It Is My Honor to Represent Them'." Last modified Jan 20, 2019, 2019. Accessed May 24, 2024. https://www.wlwt.com/article/rep-massie-defends-cov-cath-students-its-my-honor-to-represent-them/25970945.

"State of Alabama V. M. L. King, Jr., Nos. 7399 and 9593." Stanford University (The Martin Luther King, Jr. Research and Education Institute). Accessed May 24, 2024. https://kinginstitute.stanford.edu/state-alabama-v-m-l-king-jr-nos-7399-and-9593.

"Understanding Meta's Fact-Checking Program." 2023. Accessed May 24, 2024. https://www.facebook.com/government-nonprofits/blog/misinformation-resources#:~:text=Meta%20started%20its%20fact%2Dchecking,are%20timely%2C%20trending%20and%20consequential.

"Understanding the Difference between Fact and Opinion." *Financial Crime Academy*, May 24, 20242024. https://financialcrimeacademy.org/difference-between-fact-and-opinion/.

"Us Author Loses Book Deal for Tweet-Shaming." Last modified May 13, 2019, 2019. Accessed May 24, 2024. https://www.bbc.com/news/world-us-canada-48257825.

2024. "Intellectual Foundations of the American Founding." Accessed May 24, 2024. https://constitutioncenter.org/the-constitution/historic-document-library/time-period/intellectual-foundations.

Aharonoff, Daniel. "The Landmark Case That Redefined Free Speech: Analyzing Nyt V. Sullivan." Last modified Jan 3, 2024, 2024. Accessed May 24, 2024. https://www.aharonofftechtales.com/2024/01/the-landmark-case-that-redefined-free.html.

Alexander Hamilton, James Madison, Clinton Rossiter, John Jay, and Charles Kesler. *The Federalist Papers*: New York: Signet Classics, and imprint of New American Library a division of Penguin Group (USA), 2005.

Association, Kentucky Distillers'. "Kentucky Bourbon Trail Trip Planner." 2024. Accessed May 24, 2024. https://kybourbontrail.com/itineraries/kentucky-bourbon-trail/.

Batchelor, James. "Shipwright Studios Cuts Ties with Tripwire Interactive over President's Anti-Abortion Views." Last modified Sep 6, 2021, 2021. Accessed May 24, 2024. https://www.gamesindustry.biz/shipwright-studios-cuts-ties-with-tripwire-interactive-over-presidents-anti-abortion-views.

Beam, Adam, and Brian Melley. "Students in 'Maga' Hats Mock Native American after Rally." Last modified Jan 20, 2019, 2019. Accessed May 24, 2024. https://www.pbs.org/newshour/nation/students-in-maga-hats-mock-native-american-after-rally.

Boyd, Jordan. "Idaho Cop Suspended for Viral Tiktok Mocking Lebron James' Police Threat." Last modified Apr 29, 2021, 2021. Accessed May 24, 2024. https://thefederalist.com/2021/04/29/idaho-cop-suspended-for-viral-tiktok-mocking-lebron-james-police-threat/.

Britzky, Haley. "Everything Trump Has Called "Fake News"." Last modified Jul 9, 2017, 2017. Accessed May 24, 2024. https://www.axios.com/2017/12/15/everything-trump-has-called-fake-news-1513303959.

Brooks, Khristopher J. "Tripwire Interactive Ceo Steps down after Supporting Texas Abortion Law." Last modified Sep 7, 2021, 2021. Accessed May 24, 2024. https://www.cbsnews.com/news/tripwire-texas-abortion-john-gibson-gaming-tweet/.

Brown, Lee. "See Gina Carano's Tweets and Posts That Got Her Fired from 'the Mandalorian'." Last modified Feb 11, 2021, 2021. Accessed May 24, 2024. https://nypost.com/2021/02/11/see-gina-caranos-tweets-and-posts-that-got-her-fired/.

ChatGPT. *Response to Sandmann Review*. OpenAI, 2024.

Chiu, Elizabeth. "The Legacy of Rehtaeh Parsons." CBC News. 2018. Accessed May 24, 2024. https://newsinteractives.cbc.ca/longform/five-years-gone/.

Choi, Annette. "Record Number of Anti-Lgbtq Bills Were Introduced in 2023." Last modified Jan 22, 2024, 2023. Accessed May 24, 2024. https://www.cnn.com/politics/anti-lgbtq-plus-state-bill-rights-dg/index.html.

Paul Bunyan. Walt Disney, 1958. 17:00.

Cole, Liam. "Former Trump Spokesman Launches New Social Media Platform Gettr." News Nation USA. 2021. Accessed May 24, 2024. https://web.archive.org/web/20211021192931/https://

newsnationusa.com/uncategorized/former-trump-spokesman-launches-new-social-media-platform-gettr/.

Cooper, Ryan. "Fact Check: Covid-19 Not Being Blamed for Deaths Primarily Due to Unrelated Causes." Last modified Apr 1, 2020, 2020. Accessed May 24, 2024. https://leadstories.com/hoax-alert/2020/04/Fact-Check-COVID19-NOT-Being-Blamed-For-Deaths-Primarily-Due-To-Unrelated-Causes.html.

Deadspin. "Sinclair's Soldiers in Trump's War on Media". YouTube Video. 2018, 1:38. https://www.youtube.com/watch?v=_fHfgU8oMSo.

Doyle, Katherine. "Icymi: Nbc News – Rep. Elise Stefanik Files Ethics Complaint against Judge in Trump's Civil Fraud Trial." 2023. Accessed May 24, 2024. https://eliseforcongress.com/2023/11/10/icymi-nbc-news-rep-elise-stefanik-files-ethics-complaint-against-judge-in-trumps-civil-fraud-trial/.

Facebook. "Understanding Meta's Fact-Checking Program." 2023. Accessed May 24, 2024. https://www.facebook.com/government-nonprofits/blog/misinformation-resources.

Fernandez, Lance. "Who Is Carron J. Phillips? Deadspin Writer under Fire for Accusing Chiefs Fan of Blackface and Racism." Last modified Nov 29, 2023, 2023. Accessed May 24, 2024. https://www.msn.com/en-us/sports/nfl/who-is-carron-j-phillips-deadspin-writer-under-fire-for-accusing-chiefs-fan-of-blackface-and-racism/ar-AA1kIhxe.

Fischler, Jacob. "Updated: The Trump Indictments: A Seven-Year Timeline of Key Developments." Last modified May 14, 2024, 2023. Accessed May 24, 2024. https://penncapital-star.com/campaigns-elections/updated-the-trump-indictments-a-seven-year-timeline-of-key-developments/.

Gettys, Travis. "'Threatening Their Livelihood': Democrats Target Pro-Trump Attorneys for Disbarment." Last modified Mar 7, 2022, 2022. Accessed May 24, 2024. https://www.rawstory.com/the-65-project/.

Goldberg, Kevin. "Perspective: Why Arguments for Regulating Social Media Fail the First Amendment Test." Freedom Forum. Accessed May 2024, 2024. https://www.freedomforum.org/social-media-regulation-first-amendment/.

Hallmark, Kirsten. "Death by Words: Do United States Statutes Hold Cyberbullies Liable for Their Victims' Suicide?" Houston Law Review. 2023. Accessed May 24, 2024. https://houstonlawreview.org/article/73672-death-by-words-do-united-states-statutes-hold-cyberbullies-liable-for-their-victims-suicide.

Harris, Allison P., and Maya Sen. "Bias and Judging." *Annual Review of Political Science* 22 (28 May 2019: 241-59. https://ssrn.com/abstract=3394078.

Herlihy, Brianna. "Legal Experts Say Trump's Whopping New York Fee Could Be 'Excessive' under Constitution: 'Unheard Of'." Last modified Mar 26, 2024, 2024. Accessed May 24, 2024. https://www.foxnews.com/politics/legal-experts-say-trumps-whopping-new-york-fee-could-be-excessive-under-constitution-unheard-of.

Hod, Itay, and Jon Levine. "Https://Www.Thewrap.Com/Film-Producer-Jack-Morrissey-Apologizes-for-Deleted-Covington-Woodchipper-Tweet/." Last modified Jan 21, 2019, 2019. Accessed May 24, 2024. https://www.thewrap.com/film-producer-jack-morrissey-apologizes-for-deleted-covington-woodchipper-tweet/.

Holloway, Daniel. "Lucasfilm, Uta Drop 'Mandalorian' Star Gina Carano Following Offensive Social Media Posts." Last modified Feb 10, 2021, 2021. Accessed May 24, 2024. https://variety.com/2021/tv/news/mandalorian-gina-carano-1234905589/.

Izaguirre, Anthony. "Ny Attorney General Letitia James Has a Long History of Fighting Trump and Other Powerful Targets." Last modified Sept 28, 2023, 2023. Accessed May 24, 2024. https://www.usnews.com/

news/politics/articles/2023-09-28/ny-attorney-general-letitia-james-has-a-long-history-of-fighting-trump-other-powerful-targets.

James, LeBron (@KingJames). "Anger Does Any of Us ...." X (Twitter), Apr 21, 2021, 2021. https://x.com/KingJames/status/1385011051087810561.

James, LeBron (@KingJames). "I'm So Damn Tired ...." X (Twitter), Apr 21, 2021, 2021. https://x.com/KingJames/status/1385013333007343619.

Journalists, Society of Professional. "Code of Ethics." (2014). https://www.spj.org/pdf/spj-code-of-ethics.pdf.

Katherine Faulders, John Santucci, Lucien Bruggeman, and Alexander Mallin. "Trump Hit with Sweeping Indictment in Alleged Effort to Overturn 2020 Election." ABC News. 2023. Accessed May 2024, 2024. https://abcnews.go.com/US/trump-indicted-charges-related-efforts-overturn-2020-election/story?id=101612810.

Keneally, Meghan. "List of Trump's Accusers and Their Allegations of Sexual Misconduct." Last modified Sep 18, 2020, 2020. Accessed May 24, 2024. https://abcnews.go.com/Politics/list-trumps-accusers-allegations-sexual-misconduct/story?id=51956410.

Kim, Eun Kyung. "Nick Sandmann on Encounter with Nathan Phillips: 'I Wish I Would've Walked Away'." Last modified Jan 23, 2019, 2019. Accessed May 24, 2024. https://www.today.com/news/nick-sandmann-interview-today-show-s-savannah-guthrie-encounter-native-t147242.

Kyle Cheney, Andrew Desiderio, and John Bresnahan. "Trump Acquitted on Impeachment Charges, Ending Gravest Threat to His Presidency." Politico. Last modified February 5, 2020, 2020. Accessed May 2024, 2024. https://www.politico.com/news/2020/02/05/trump-impeachment-vote-110805.

Life, March for (@March_for_Life). X (Twitter), 6:48 PM · Jan 20, 2019, 2019. https://x.com/March_for_Life/status/1087179995414519810.

Mascaro, Lisa, Mary Clare Jalonick, Jonathan Lemire, and Alan Fram. "Trump Impeached after Capitol Riot in Historic Second Charge." Last modified Jan 13, 2021, 2021. Accessed May 24, 2024. https://apnews.com/article/trump-impeachment-vote-capitol-siege-0a6f2a348a6e43f27d5e1dc486027860.

Merriam-Webster.com. "Definition of Defamation." Merriam Webster. Last modified 14 May 2024. Accessed May 24, 2024. https://www.merriam-webster.com/dictionary/defamation.

Mitchell, Amy, Jeffrey Gottfried, Galen Stocking, Mason Walker, and Sophia Fedeli. "Many Americans Say Made-up News Is a Critical Problem That Needs to Be Fixed." Pew Research Center. 2019. Accessed May 24, 2024. https://www.pewresearch.org/journalism/2019/06/05/many-americans-say-made-up-news-is-a-critical-problem-that-needs-to-be-fixed/.

Morrison, Sara. "Section 230, the Internet Law the Supreme Court Could Change, Explained." Maverick Studios. Last modified February 23, 2023, 2020. Accessed May 24, 2024. https://maverickstudios.net/2023/02/23/section-230-the-internet-law-the-supreme-court-could-change-explained/.

Moses, Toby. "Gina Carano Fired from the Mandalorian after 'Abhorrent' Social Media Posts." Last modified Feb 11, 2021, 2021. Accessed May 24, 2024. https://www.theguardian.com/tv-and-radio/2021/feb/11/gina-carano-fired-from-the-mandalorian-after-abhorrent-social-media-posts.

Mustian, Jim. "New York Court Suspends Rudy Giuliani's Law License." Last modified June 24, 2021, 2021. Accessed May 24, 2024. https://apnews.com/article/rudy-giuliani-new-york-law-license-suspended-c67f4504a22f8642d6096f29e3a5c51e.

Nashrulla, Tasneem. "The Writer Who Lost Her Book Deal after Calling out a Dc Metro Worker for Eating on the Train Is Suing the Publisher for

$13 Million." Last modified Jun 9, 2019, 2019. Accessed May 24, 2024. https://www.buzzfeednews.com/article/tasneemnashrulla/dc-metro-writer-tweet-eating-train-book-sue-publisher.

Novak, Daniel, and Sara Shayanian. "Rhetorical Hyperbole Is the Defamation Defense Du Jour (Guest Column)." Last modified April 14, 2021, 2021. Accessed May 24, 2024. https://www.hollywoodreporter.com/business/business-news/rhetorical-hyperbole-is-the-defamation-defense-du-jour-guest-column-4166328/.

Oremus, Will. "Tech Giants Banned Trump. But Did They Censor Him?" Last modified Jan 7, 2022, 2022. Accessed May 24, 2024. https://www.washingtonpost.com/technology/2022/01/07/trump-facebook-ban-censorship/.

Orr, Gabby, Kristen Holmes, and Veronica Stracqualursi. "Former President Donald Trump Announces a White House Bid for 2024." Last modified Nov 16, 2022, 2022. Accessed May 24, 2024. https://www.cnn.com/2022/11/15/politics/trump-2024-presidential-bid/index.html.

Owens, Candace. "According to Cdc Reports...." Meta (Facebook)2020. https://www.facebook.com/realCandaceOwens/photos/according-to-cdc-reports-2020-is-working-out-to-be-the-lowest-flu-death-season-o/3701927883211719/.

Owens, Candace (@RealCandaceO). "Guess What?!" X (Twitter), Nov 5, 2020, 2020. https://x.com/RealCandaceO/status/1324515021657812992.

Owens, Candace. "Important Information for Everyone to Know About...." Meta (Facebook), March 29, 2020, 2020. https://www.facebook.com/realCandaceOwens/posts/3598900840181091.

Owens, Candace (@RealCandaceO). "Possibly the Greatest Trade Deal Ever...." X (Twitter), Apr 28, 2020, 2020. https://twitter.com/RealCandaceO/status/1255138389080203267.

Pedroja, Cammy. "Nate Silvester, Cop Who Mocked Lebron James, Fired for Violating City and State Policies." Lipstick Alley. 2021. Accessed May 24, 2024. https://www.lipstickalley.com/threads/nate-silvester-cop-who-mocked-lebron-james-fired-for-violating-city-and-state-policies.4558658/.

Pelchen, Lexie. "Internet Usage Statistics in 2024." Last modified Mar 1, 2024, 2024. Accessed May 24, 2024. https://www.forbes.com/home-improvement/internet/internet-statistics/.

Perry, Tod. "Writer's Career in Jeopardy after Tweeting About a Black Metro Worker Eating on the Train." Last modified May 20, 2019, 2019. Accessed May 24, 2024. https://www.upworthy.com/writer-s-career-in-jeopardy-after-tweeting-about-a-black-metro-worker-eating-on-the-train.

Phillips, Carron J. "The Nfl Must Ban Native Headdress and Culturally Insensitive Face Paint in the Stands (Updated)." 2023. Accessed May 24, 2024. https://deadspin.com/roger-goodell-kansas-city-chiefs-fan-black-face-native-1851048905/.

Reilly, Katie. "The Viral Lincoln Memorial Confrontation Shows We're Ill-Equipped to Deal with Online Disinformation." Last modified Jan 23, 2019, 2019. Accessed May 24, 2024. https://time.com/5509832/covington-catholic-nathan-phillips-social-media-division/.

Richardson, Valerie. "Reza Aslan 'Likely' to Be Sued over Now-Deleted 'Punchable Face' Tweet: Sandmann Attorney." Last modified Jan 13, 2020, 2020. Accessed May 24, 2024. https://www.washingtontimes.com/news/2020/jan/13/reza-aslan-likely-be-sued-over-now-deleted-punchab/.

Rueb, Sarah Mervosh and Emily S. "Fuller Picture Emerges of Viral Video of Native American Man and Catholic Students." The New York Times. 2019. Accessed May 2024, 2024. https://www.nytimes.com/2019/01/20/us/nathan-phillips-covington.html.

Sarkar, Alisha Rahaman. "Tech Ceo and Self-Proclaimed 'Pro-Life Gamer' Steps down after Backing Texas Abortion Law." Independent. Last modified Tuesday 07 September 2021, 2021. Accessed May 24, 2024. https://www.independent.co.uk/news/world/americas/tripwire-ceo-texas-abortion-law-b1915476.html.

Schmad, Robert. "Fact Check: Nearly 100 Percent of Political Contributions from Fact Checkers Go to Democrats." Last modified Jun 13, 2023, 2023. Accessed May 24, 2024. https://freebeacon.com/media/fact-check-nearly-100-percent-of-political-contributions-from-fact-checkers-go-to-democrats/.

Scholl, Jacob. "That Idaho Police Officer's Video About Lebron James? His Employer Isn't Happy About It." Last modified Apr 29, 2021, 2021. Accessed May 24, 2024. https://www.idahostatesman.com/news/northwest/idaho/article251037234.html.

Schonfeld, Ariel, Dale McNiel, Takeo Toyoshima, and Renée Binder. "Cyberbullying and Adolescent Suicide." *Journal of the American Academy of Psychiatry and the Law Online* (2023): JAAPL.220078-22. https://dx.doi.org/10.29158/jaapl.220078-22.

Shepherd, Joanna, and Michael S. Kang. "Partisan Justice." Accessed May 24, 2024. https://www.acslaw.org/analysis/reports/partisan-justice/.

Simons, Daniel. "Selective Attention Test". YouTube Video. 2010, 1:21. https://www.youtube.com/watch?v=vJG698U2Mvo.

Smolla, Rodney A. *Law of Defamation.* 2 vols. Second Edition ed. Eagan, MN: Thomson Reuters, 1999.

Society, Federalist. "About Us." Federalist Society. 2024. Accessed May 24, 2024. https://fedsoc.org/about-us#Background.

Southern, Matt G. "Elon Musk's Twitter Takeover: A Timeline of Events." Last modified Nov 16, 2022, 2022. Accessed May 24, 2024.

https://www.searchenginejournal.com/elon-musks-twitter-takeover-a-timeline-of-events/470927/.

Triggernometry. "An Honest Conversation with Ben Shapiro". YouTube Video. 2023, 1:04:00. https://www.youtube.com/watch?v=HM282oySNbM.

Valdes, Elpidio. "Fox News: State Television and Propaganda." Last modified Apr 29, 2022, 2022. Accessed May 24, 2024. https://elpidio.org/2022/04/29/fox-news-state-television-and-propaganda/.

Walsh, Math. "Matt Walsh's Apology to the Left". Oct 6, 2022. YouTube Video. 2022, 15:21. https://www.youtube.com/watch?v=WGWOo0fj7uk.

Weber, Peter. "What Do the Democrats Stand For?" Last modified Oct 9, 2023, 2023. Accessed May 24, 2024. https://theweek.com/politics/what-do-the-democrats-stand-for.

Weiner, Rachel. "Rudy Giuliani Suspended from Practicing Law in D.C. Court." Last modified Jul 7, 2021, 2021. Accessed May 24, 2024. https://www.washingtonpost.com/local/legal-issues/giuliani-washington-court/2021/07/07/9f7a7f5c-df6a-11eb-9f54-7eee10b5fcd2_story.html.

Whitcomb, Dan. "Former U.S. President Donald Trump Launches 'Truth' Social Media Platform." Last modified April 30, 2024, 2021. Accessed May 24, 2024. https://www.reuters.com/world/us/former-us-president-donald-trump-launches-new-social-media-platform-2021-10-21/.

Wiggins, Christopher. "Msnbc's Decision Not to Air Trump's Iowa Victory Speech Live Ignites Right-Wing Firestorm." Last modified Jan 17, 2024, 2024. Accessed May 24, 2024. https://www.advocate.com/media/rachel-maddow-trump-iowa-speech.

Wilder, Drew, Jackie Bensen, and Andrea Swalec. "'The Meeting Has Degenerated': 1 Arrest, 1 Injury at Loudoun Schools Meeting on Equity." Last modified Jun 23, 2021, 2021. Accessed May 24, 2024. https://

www.nbcwashington.com/news/local/northern-virginia/loudoun-school-board-transgender-student-policy-race-equity/2708185/.

Williams, David, and Emanuella Grinberg. "Teen in Confrontation with Native American Elder Says He Was Trying to Defuse the Situation." Last modified Jan 23, 2019, 2019. Accessed MAY 24, 2024. https://www.cnn.com/2019/01/19/us/teens-mock-native-elder-trnd/index.html.

Winter, Ree. "The Accusation That Had Tiktok Spamming a Restaurant with Bad Reviews." Last modified July 8, 2022, 2022. Accessed May 24, 2024. https://www.mashed.com/921822/the-accusation-that-had-tiktok-spamming-a-restaurant-with-bad-reviews/.

Wuinn, Melissa, and Graham Kates. "Trump's 4 Indictments in Detail: A Quick-Look Guide to Charges, Trial Dates and Key Players for Each Case." Last modified May 9, 2024, 2024. Accessed May 24, 2024. https://www.cbsnews.com/news/trump-indictments-details-guide-charges-trial-dates-people-case/.

Yurcaba, Jo. "Over 30 New Lgbtq Education Laws Are in Effect as Students Go Back to School." Last modified Aug 30, 2023, 2023. Accessed May 24, 2024. https://www.nbcnews.com/nbc-out/out-politics-and-policy/30-new-lgbtq-education-laws-are-effect-students-go-back-school-rcna101897.

Defiance. Paramount Pictures, 2008. 137 mins.

Made in the USA
Monee, IL
21 November 2024

70771005R00173